"There have been a ton of books written on governance and best practices for boards since corporate reform post-Enron increased the scrutiny on directors. **SIMPLY PUT: THIS IS ONE THAT IS DEFINITELY WORTH READING!**"

> T. K. KERSTETTER
> President, *Corporate Board Member*

"Drawing on an extensive array of research and current events, the authors present **AN EXCELLENT EXAMPLE OF THE KIND OF WORK THAT WILL BE NECESSARY TO IMPROVE THE CURRENT STATE OF CORPORATE GOVERNANCE** in the United States. Mindful of the importance that trust and fiduciary duty play in the integrity of our free enterprise system, the book outlines a clarion call to regulators, directors, and executives to become active participants in reforming our corporate governance system."

> RAKESH KHURANA
> Assistant Professor, Harvard Business School
> Author, *Searching for a Corporate Savior: The Irrational Quest for Charismatic CEOs*

"In *Putting Investors First,* Scott Newquist and Max Russell clearly outline the why and how of good corporate governance and convincingly argue for a return of integrity and trust in the boardroom. The corporate scandals of recent years have taught us that corporate governance matters. Newquist and Russell now teach us how to make it real. **IN ADDITION TO ALL THE NEW LEGAL AND REGULATORY REQUIREMENTS IMPOSED ON CORPORATE BOARD MEMBERS, ADD ONE: READ THIS BOOK!**"

> LINDA E. SCOTT
> Director of Corporate Governance, TIAA-CREF
> Former Director of Investor Affairs, NYS Common Retirement Fund

"This book addresses the most important aspects of corporate governance. It's direct and very pointed in its observations about how to improve corporate governance, as well as practical in how to avoid topics and issues that are not essential to making the board function well. **IT'S A PRACTICAL, HANDS-ON, AND INSIGHTFUL WORK.**"

BETSY ATKINS
Corporate Governance Specialist
CEO of Baja Ventures

"**THIS IS A TERRIFIC BOOK.** It takes on one of the most-timely topics of the day—the failure of modern corporate governance to protect shareholder interests—and speaks candidly with a genuineness born of Scott Newquist's personal experience as an investment banker and board adviser. The writing is lively and straightforward, and the whole book is a clarion call for corporate boards to wake up."

MICHAEL E. YOUNG
Partner, Willkie Farr & Gallagher
Author, *Accounting Irregularities and Financial Fraud*

PUTTING INVESTORS
FIRST

PUTTING INVESTORS
FIRST

REAL SOLUTIONS FOR
BETTER CORPORATE GOVERNANCE

Scott C. Newquist
with Max B. Russell

Bloomberg PRESS

P R I N C E T O N

First edition published 2003

1 3 5 7 9 10 8 6 4 2

Library of Congress Cataloging-in-Publication Data

Newquist, Scott C.
  Putting investors first: real solutions for better corporate governance / Scott C. Newquist with Max B. Russell. – 1st ed.
    p. cm.
Includes bibliographical references and index.
  ISBN 1-57660-141-2 (alk. paper)
  1. Corporate governance–United States. 2. Boards of directors–United States. 3. Corporations–Investor relations. I. Russell, Max B. II. Title.

HD2741.N58 2003
658.4'2–dc21   2003008181

Acquired by KATHLEEN PETERSON
Book design by BARBARA DIEZ GOLDENBERG

To Aileen, my wife, love, and lifetime partner

CONTENTS

.

ACKNOWLEDGMENTS

ALTHOUGH THEY ARE TOO NUMEROUS for me to mention them all by name, I want thank the many directors, CEOs, and other executives at corporations, mutual funds, and pension funds who have allowed me to use them as sounding boards for the concepts in this book. Sometimes they agreed with me, sometimes not. Nonetheless, they have been extraordinarily gracious in giving me their time and have proved invaluable in confirming the issues that exist and sharing their experiences in addressing them. A few individuals deserve special mention for their contributions: Bill Cotter of AIG, Michael Young of Willkie Farr and Gallagher, Michael Mitrione of Gunster Yokely and Stewart, and Gerald Czarnecki of the teaching faculty of the National Association of Corporate Directors, who has been a valued adviser. A special word of thanks also to Jack Bogle for his commitment to better corporate governance, his excellent ideas and counsel, and his thoughtful foreword to this work.

Books don't write themselves, so I'm especially grateful to my business partner of thirteen years, Robert G. Eccles, who encouraged me to write this book, helped me to apply transparency concepts and approaches to governance, and who also introduced me to Max Russell, whose superb writing skills helped to bring this story to life. I am grateful to Kathleen Peterson of Bloomberg Press for championing this book and to our editor at Bloomberg, Chris Miles, for bringing clarity and conciseness to our writing.

I would also like to express my thanks to several employees of Board Governance Services: Jeff Heath, who worked tirelessly gathering information, analyzing issues, and offering excellent ideas; Laura Pohle, whose research abilities and attention to detail made our job so much easier; and Sally Evans, whose organizational skills and administrative talents helped keep us moving forward.

Finally, I thank my wife, Aileen Newquist, for listening to my ideas at all hours of the day and night, challenging them, adding value to the content, and reviewing our work again and again— her patience is exceptional. And to my daughters Peyton and Paige: Your understanding and love have supported me always.

SCOTT C. NEWQUIST

FOREWORD

BY JOHN C. BOGLE
FOUNDER AND FORMER CEO OF THE VANGUARD GROUP

OUR AMERICAN SYSTEM of corporate governance is facing one
of the greatest challenges in its history. If it is fair to say—and I
think it is—that the system is under attack, it is corporate directors who are bearing the brunt of much of the heavy artillery. The
integrity of our system has clearly been violated by particular
cases of egregious misfeasance and even fraud. Our regulators
and enforcement authorities are targeting these so-called "bad
apples" and striking them with no mean precision. But there are
also a lot of blunderbusses out there, firing away blindly at the system itself, calling attention to its weaknesses and failing, blasting
away at the very *barrel* that holds all those apples, good and bad
alike. The clear message: It is not enough to take action only
when we see specific failures. If we are to minimize the likelihood
that such failures will recur, we must improve our capitalistic system. *We need to fix the barrel.*

In the interest of full disclosure, you can place me squarely in
the camp of the authors of *Putting Investors First* and others who
believe the present system must be reformed. The first step is to
change the way that directors see themselves. For it is the directors of corporate America who have presided over what has been
called—accurately, I believe—by essayist-journalist William Pfaff
"a pathological mutation in capitalism." The classic system—
owners capitalism—had been based on a dedication to serving the
interests of the corporation's *owners* in maximizing the return on
their capital investment. But a new system developed—*managers*
capitalism—in which the corporation came to be run to profit its
managers, in complicity if not conspiracy with accountants and
the managers of other corporations. Why did it happen?

"Because," in Mr. Pfaff's words, "the markets had so diffused corporate ownership *that no responsible owner exists.* This is morally unacceptable, but also a corruption of capitalism itself."

That transmogrification—that grotesque transformation—of a system of owners capitalism into a system of managers capitalism required only two ingredients: (1) the diffusion of corporate ownership among a large number of investors, none holding a controlling share of the voting power; and (2) the unwillingness of the *agents* of the owners—the boards of directors—to honor their responsibility to serve above all else the interests of their *principals,* the shareowners themselves. Most owners either don't or won't or can't stand up for their rights, and when directors lose sight of whom they represent, the resulting power vacuum quickly gets filled by corporate managers, living proof that Spinoza was right when he told us, "nature abhors a vacuum." And that is just what we have witnessed. No, not in every corporation, but in enough corporations so that managers capitalism became a fair characterization of the system at large—the barrel itself.

Too many directors failed to consider that their overriding responsibility was to represent the largely faceless, voiceless shareholders who elected them—failed, if you will, to honor the director's golden rule: "Behave as if the corporation you serve had a single absentee owner, and do your best to further his long-term interests in all proper ways." Those words were used by Warren Buffett in his Berkshire-Hathaway Annual Report in 1993, a full decade ago. As a group, alas, our corporate directors have failed to adequately measure up to that standard.

Mr. Buffett, who has now added the not inconsiderable heft of his peerless reputation and the sharpness of his articulate commentary to the need for governance reform, also suggests three other standards for independent directors: that they be "business-savvy, interested, and shareholder-oriented," the latter of which, in Berkshire's case, means being a significant long-term shareholder of Berkshire. Even if most of us mere mortals who serve as corporate directors cannot fully meet that final standard, those three qualifications are obviously essential, too.

Put another way, it is the responsibility of those who serve on the boards of directors to ensure that the enterprise's resources are used in the faithful service of its owners—to be good stewards, if you will, of the corporate property entrusted to them. But as boards of directors turned over to the company's managers the virtually unfettered power to place their own interests first, both the word and the concept of stewardship became conspicuous by their absence from the list of values on corporate America's agenda.

The result: a raft of misleading corporate financial statements and the grotesquely excessive executive compensation that helped create the stock market bubble and—bubbles being bubbles—its subsequent burst. Yet the directors of corporate America couldn't have been unaware of the management's aggressive "earnings guidance." Nor of the focus on raising the price of the stock, never mind at what cost to the value of the corporation. Nor of the fact that the lower the dividend, the more capital the company retains. Nor that the estimated future returns of 9 percent to 10 percent or more on the company's pension fund were little more than "pie in the sky." Nor that it was management that hired the consultants who recommended to the compensation committee higher compensation for that very same management, year after year, even when its actual accomplishments in building the business were hardly out of the ordinary. Nor that shares acquired by executives through stock options were sold as soon as they vested, often with the corporation putting up the money in a "cashless exercise." Nor that the company's accounting firm was receiving consulting fees many times the amount of its auditing fees, substantially vitiating both its independence and its integrity. Surely it is fair to say that it is our corporate directors who should bear the ultimate responsibility for what went wrong with capitalism in corporate America.

But think about it for a moment. *Why* should the board bear the ultimate responsibility when it doesn't even *have* the ultimate responsibility? Of course the directors' responsibility is large indeed, but it is the stockholders themselves who bear the *ultimate* responsibility for corporate governance. And as investing has become institutionalized, stockholders have gained the *real*—as compared with the *theoretical*—power to exercise their will. Once owned largely by a diffuse and inchoate group of individual investors, each one with relatively modest holdings, today the ownership of stocks is concentrated—for better or worse!—among a remarkably small group of institutions whose potential power is truly awesome. The 100 largest managers of pension funds and mutual funds alone now represent the ownership of one-half of all U.S. equities: *absolute control over corporate America.* Together, these 100 large institutional investors constitute the great 800-pound gorilla that can sit wherever he wants to sit at the board table.

But with all that power has come little interest in corporate governance. That is an amazing disconnection between the potential and the reality—awesome power, largely unexercised. Yet institutional managers could hardly have been ignorant of what was going on in corporate America. Even before the stock market bubble burst, for example, the mutual fund industry's well-educated, highly-trained, experienced professional analysts and portfolio managers *must* have been poring over company fiscal statements; evaluating corporate plans; and measuring the extent to which long-term corporate goals were being achieved, how cash flow compared with reported earnings, and the extent to which those ever-fallacious "pro forma" earnings diverged from the fiscal reality. Yet few, if any, voices were raised. Somehow our professional investors either didn't understand, or understood but ignored—I'm not sure which is worse!—the house of cards that the stock market had become. We worshiped at the altar of the precise but ephemeral *price of the stock,* forgetting that the eternal sovereign is the intrinsic *value of the corporation*—simply the discounted value of its future cash flow.

Astonishingly, however, the reaction of institutional investors to the failings of our system has yet to occur. Even after the bear market that devastated the value of our clients' equity holdings, the only response we've heard from the mutual fund industry is the sound of silence. Why? Because the overwhelming majority of mutual funds continues to engage, not in the process of long-term investing on the basis of intrinsic corporate *values,* but in the process of short-term speculation based on momentary stock *prices.* How else could one fairly describe an investment policy in which the average fund portfolio turns over at 110 percent per year, with the average fund holding the average stock for an average of but eleven months? The typical fund manager has lots of interest in a company's price momentum—its quarterly earnings and whether or not it is meeting the guidance given to Wall Street. But when it comes to what a company is actually worth—its fundamental earning power, its balance sheet, its long-term strategy, its intrinsic value—there seems to be far less interest. When Oscar Wilde described the cynic as "a man who knows the price of everything but the value of nothing," he could have as easily been talking about fund managers.

What's Been Done

IF THE CHANGE — "the pathological mutation," if you will—from owners capitalism to managers capitalism is the root cause of the grave failings of our system in the recent era, what's to be done? The first order of business is to recognize that we need not only good *managers* of corporate America, but good *owners.* And we need owners and managers to work together to restore the integrity of the system. Much work has already been done:

- **Regulation.** The SEC has aggressively undertaken an impressive array of sound regulatory changes and enforcement actions, and the Justice Department is opening up criminal investigations. We can all hope that severe punishment is meted out to those who have abrogated the trust placed in them and violated the law.

- **Legislation.** We have Sarbanes-Oxley, and with it the Public Company Accounting Oversight Board. Whether or not the law has gone too far and placed too much emphasis on form over substance, my own view is that we now have most of the legislation we need, at least for the moment.

- **The financial markets.** The New York Stock Exchange, and then Nasdaq, have established powerful and extensive sets of mandatory governance practices for their listed corporations, designed to strengthen board independence and set new standards for audit committees and compensation committees.
- **The public sector.** When things "go to seed" in America, it is only a short time until good citizens respond by forming themselves into commissions to recommend remedial action. And as the evidence of substantial financial malfeasance began to emerge, The Conference Board formed its "Blue Ribbon Commission on Public Trust and Private Enterprise" which has already produced a substantial "white paper" with wide variety of policy recommendations, including tackling head-on some of the toughest, most contentious issues of the day: Stock options should be expensed, the offices of Chairman of the Board and CEO should be separated, auditors should perform no consulting services for their clients, to name just three of the 73(!) specific "Best Practice" recommendations set forth by the Commission. This group included such luminaries as cochairmen Peter G. Peterson and John Snow, Paul Volcker, Arthur Levitt, Warren Rudman, and John Biggs.

What's to Be Done

BUT THERE'S MUCH MORE to be done, and it will not be easy. What capitalism needs most of all is a return to a focus on long-term *investing*. Our very society depends on it, for our economic growth depends upon capital formation. Way back in 1936, Lord Keynes warned us, "When enterprise becomes a mere bubble on a whirlpool of speculation, the position is serious. *For when the capital development of a country becomes a by-product of the activities of a casino, the job is likely to be ill-done.*" As a nation we can't afford to let that happen. The fact is that we need a whole new mindset for institutional investors, one in which *speculation* becomes a mere bubble on a whirlpool of *investment*. In the mutual fund industry, we need to go "back to the future," to return to our traditional focus on stewardship, and to abandon the focus on salesmanship that has dominated our recent history.

But the fact of the matter is that we need *both* good owners *and* good managers, with both sides working in concert. How to begin? Here are six suggestions:

Improve corporate citizenship. Investors—and particularly institutional investors—will become better owners only if we at last return to behaving as responsible corporate citizens, voting our proxies thoughtfully and communicating our views to corporate managements. The SEC's recent decision to require mutual funds to disclose how we vote our proxies is a long overdue first step in getting more involvement in governance from mutual fund managers. The next step must be to give substantial investors "access" to corporate proxy statements, so we can place both nominations for directors and business proposals *directly* in the corporate proxies.

Clearly separate ownership from management. To help institutional owners implement a greater focus on governance, corporations should have an independent board chairman and higher standards of director independence. Also, the board should have access to independent advisers or even a small staff to provide them with information on compensation, accounting, and other matters that is without management bias.

Return to a long-term focus. Owners and managers must unite in returning the focus of corporate information to long-term financial goals, cash flows, intrinsic values, and strategic direction. The pernicious quarterly "earnings guidance," so omnipresent today, should be *eliminated*. So should efforts to meet financial targets through creative accounting techniques.

Let sunlight shine on accounting. Given the enormous latitude accorded by "Generally Accepted Accounting Principles," owners must demand, and managers must provide, full disclosure of the impact of significant accounting policy decisions. Indeed, maybe we ought to require that corporations report earnings not only on a "most aggressive" basis (presumably what they are reporting today), but on a "most conservative" basis as well.

Provide tax incentives. We need differential tax strategies aimed at stemming excessive speculation. Some years ago, Warren Buffett suggested a 100 percent tax on short-term capital gains, paid not only by taxable investors, *but also by tax-exempt pension funds.* Although that tax rate *might* seem a tad extreme, perhaps a 50 percent tax on very short-term gains on trading stocks would help bring investors to their senses.

Bring back dividends. History tells us that higher dividend payouts are actually associated with *higher* future returns on stocks. Yet despite the absence of any evidence that retained earnings are used wisely by management, the payout rate has been declining for years. To state the obvious, investing for income is a *long-term* strategy and investing for capital gains is a *short-term* strategy. (Turnover of dividend-paying stocks is only half the rate of non-dividend-paying stocks.) A return of dividends to their formerly high standing on the agenda of stock owners would do much to reduce turnover and excessive speculation.

Values, Ideals, and Goodness

TOGETHER, THESE STEPS would forcefully continue the wave of reform in corporate governance and help turn America's capital development process away from speculation and toward enterprise. But there's even more at stake than improving the *practices* of governance and investing. We must also establish a higher set of *principles.* This nation's founding fathers believed in high moral standards, in a just society, and in the virtuous conduct of our affairs. Those beliefs shaped the very character of our nation. If *character counts*—and I have absolutely no doubt that character *does* count—the ethical failings of today's business and financial model, the manipulation of financial statements, the willingness of those of us in the field of investment management to accept practices that we knew were wrong, the conformity that kept us silent, the selfishness that let our greed overwhelm our reason, all eroded the character of capitalism. Yet character is what we'll need most in the years ahead, more than ever in the wake of this great bear market and the investor disenchantment it reflects, more than ever in the troubled international world around us, where America's strength lies more than ever in her values, her ideals, her goodness.

The motivations of those who seek the rewards earned by engaging in commerce and finance struck the imagination of no less a man than Adam Smith as "something grand and beautiful and noble, well worth the toil and anxiety." It's hard to imagine that anyone would use those words to describe what capitalism has been about in the recent era. The sooner we can again apply those words to our business and financial leaders—and mean them—the better.

INTRODUCTION

THE YEAR WAS 1981. I was a thirty-three-year-old outside financial adviser making a presentation to a Fortune 100 company's high-level executives—most of them in their sixties. I described for them in detail how the company's earnings per share could be increased by more than 10 percent the following year by making, structuring, and accounting for an acquisition in a certain way. The CEO, CFO, and several division heads asked questions about how events were likely to unfold, and then the executives made the decision to proceed with the deal. Because the company's board of directors had engaged the firm I represented, I asked about the need for board approval. The CEO assured me that the board would vote to confirm the decision that this group had just made.

I felt we were all on the same team. But these executives began to lecture me (a temporary agent in their decision making) in a good-natured but critical tone. They insisted that their real work—creating value for shareholders—would begin soon after the deal was closed, and long after I had gone on to structure another deal somewhere else. While they were making and delivering real products, they told me, I was just providing financial advice. Of course, they were right on both counts. At the same time, however, their immediate interest was to boost short-term earnings per share, and holding forth to me was probably as much for their own benefit as mine. They were not confident that the deal would really create value, but they knew it would increase reported earnings.

At the time, I felt that these individuals were model executives. They were smart, hard working, dedicated to their jobs, and committed to the company's success. They would never have thought of doing anything other than what they believed would ultimately benefit their company and its shareholders. Their intentions were good, but they had overlooked one very important consideration: By putting short-term results ahead of long-term value, they had failed to put investors' interests first.

Lessons I Have Learned

THIS EARLY EXPERIENCE is just one of the hundreds of interactions that I have had with executives and boards of directors in scores of companies. That exposure sparked in me a deep, long-standing interest in studying corporate governance and analyzing how and why companies (and the individuals that govern them) make decisions. I have learned that those who can achieve short-term gain, whether or not real value is created, are prized because their results can be measured immediately by those who want action. For example, executives who complete many acquisitions tend to be paid better than those who run their businesses well. Those who report superior short-term results are paid better than those who create real long-term value.

I have learned that executives—driven in varying degrees by a self standard of excellence, money, power, and stature—are extremely dedicated to the success of their companies while they are running them. They work very hard under enormous pressure. They deserve to be paid handsomely. The vast majority try to do a great job. Many succeed when measured against most performance dimensions, while clearly failing on others. Most would work just as hard in the absence of a large incentive compensation component. More often than not, incentive compensation changes behavior negatively as executives make trade-offs between qualifying for incentive pay and doing what is right for shareholders, employees, and other stakeholders.

I have learned that directors who sit on the boards of companies bring a diverse range of experience and general knowledge to their fiduciary positions. They are a valuable but greatly underutilized asset. They serve at the pleasure of the CEO, have limited time and resources to do their jobs, and seldom have sufficiently detailed knowledge of the company to challenge or question management's proposals. Even the best boards are sometimes less effective than investors would hope.

As we are all a product of our experiences, a bit of autobiography may be useful in understanding where the ideas in this book originated. I graduated Phi Beta Kappa from Williams College in 1971 with a B.A. in economics and became a lending officer at Morgan Guaranty Trust Company. Morgan's accounting training program, taught by Sandy Burton from Columbia University, was excellent and focused on how to spot when financial statements were hiding the truth. One would have thought that borrowers had been trying to put one over on lenders forever. They have.

I spent the next couple of years in the M.B.A. program at The Harvard Business School, graduating in 1975 as a George F. Baker Scholar. Probably the most valuable lesson I learned at Harvard was that discussion and debate usually result in the best answer. No matter how sure I was of the position I had taken, other opinions and judgments invariably added to my perspective. Sometimes I found I was just plain wrong.

Following Harvard, I spent two years back at Morgan Guaranty lending money to the new technology companies in Silicon Valley. Then I went to work in mergers and acquisitions at Morgan Stanley & Company. M&A was just getting started as a real business at investment banks, and Morgan Stanley was the leader. Businesses that had been less than optimally managed (and that had accumulated excess, underutilized assets) were being challenged by both external takeovers and by new leaders. This positive development increased productivity and return on capital and labor. It would not have happened without the investment banks that provided capital and the incentive to change business practices.

At the same time, investment banks that had previously respected the historic relationships of their competitors' "house clients" began to actively solicit them from one another. Competition resulted in innovation. I argued for, founded, and managed a group at Morgan Stanley called the Transactions Development Group, the purpose of which was to present acquisition ideas and structures to prospective corporate clients to win their business. We tried to put companies into play in order to earn M&A fees. Some deals created value for shareholders, and others did not.

The idea that a group of relatively young, inexperienced investment bankers could, based on their analysis of strategic fit, synergy, or cost saving, succeed in convincing the management and board of a company to buy another company was pretty ludicrous. We knew little about the details of the businesses we were advising or the ones we were suggesting they buy. In general we relied only on public information. We had little or no experience managing businesses, especially compared to the people we were advising. But we did understand how to use purchase and pooling merger accounting, how to structure securities, and how to design financials to change reported post-transaction earnings. Relying on lawyers, we knew how to create complex corporate structures to manage balance sheets. We appealed to the egos of CEOs, showing them how rapidly growing their businesses through acquisition could lead to higher pay, increased stature, and more perquisites. We were an effective catalyst for action.

A critical lesson of these experiences? Advice is influenced by and varies with the structure of compensation for that advice. Shareholders need to understand that outside, independent firms occasionally give advice to companies, but management and the board provide it daily. Their decisions are influenced by how they are paid. In terms of getting paid for giving advice, M&A advisers' compensation was based heavily on the fees paid if a deal closed. As a result, M&A advisers often focused single-mindedly on closing the deal. This same principle applies to corporate management. Even the most ethical managers are influenced by how their compensation is structured, which in turn influences the information, judgment, and advice that flow from middle management

to senior management to the CEO, and in turn from the CEO to
the board of directors.

Somewhat weary of providing advice, slightly disillusioned
with the process, and eager to become a principal in the business,
I helped persuade the leaders of Morgan Stanley to start a
Merchant Banking Group and raise a fund from outside
investors. They put me in charge of it. Having been an adviser for
many years, suddenly I became a fiduciary for investors and came
face-to-face with a major dilemma. As an employee of the firm,
my goal was to maximize my company's profitability and minimize its risk by structuring and setting the fees that investors paid.
At the same time, as a fiduciary to those investors, my goal was to
maximize their return and minimize their risk. These two ideas
created a not inconsequential conflict that is addressed throughout this book, and one that affects decision making in corporations, mutual funds, and many other organizations.

Morgan Stanley, like every other company in the industry,
charged fees based on money under management. The name of
the game across the entire industry was to buy well, but by all
means to spend the money so that more could be raised from
investors, generating more fees. From the perspective of the manager, invested funds constituted a huge option on profits from
good investments with little downside risk. If investments did not
work out, the fees were still attractive. In my opinion, Morgan
Stanley always did a better job than most in making money for
investors, protecting investors, and avoiding excesses. Although I
had been a vocal advocate for my company to enter the business,
I felt increasingly uncomfortable as a fiduciary for investors. I ran
the group for approximately three years, retiring in 1986.

In early 1988 I was recruited to turn around and build the
investment banking department of General Electric–controlled
Kidder Peabody & Company, following a period of internal tur-
moil there and at a time when the investment banking environment was terrible. The IPO market had dried up in a minireces-
sion, M&A activity was way off, and financing volume was down.
The opportunity to manage a relatively large operation within the

GE family was compelling. The next three years were not fun, but I got a great education. I learned a lot about management, meeting profitability expectations, the selective flow of information, and internal management systems. As head of investment banking I was a member of the five-person management committee with direct responsibility for corporate finance (including all industry and product groups, domestic and international operations, financial product development, M&A, real estate finance, merchant banking, high-yield securities origination and trading, public finance, and project finance).

I left Kidder Peabody in 1991 and formed an advisory company with Robert G. Eccles, formerly a tenured professor at The Harvard Business School. Our concept was that we would not just work with our clients on how to get deals done, we would also have a vested interest in whether the deals produced real value. We proposed to be paid on agreed measures of long-term value creation resulting from our advice. We also proposed to selectively put capital at risk. Our mission was to provide integrated financial, organizational, and strategic advice, including M&A, relying on the staffs of our clients to collect and analyze information so that learning would be captured by our clients instead of by the adviser. This business has prospered, but frankly we have been disappointed in the short-term focus of clients and prospective clients, and our business model has adapted to customer expectations.

Over the past five years we have become increasingly involved in transparency and disclosure issues. We have studied the varying information needs of management, research analysts, and investors on an industry-by-industry basis as well as the relative importance to each group of various types of information. Several conclusions are clear. Investors are not getting the information they want. Companies are not disclosing information that they use internally to manage their businesses and that they think is important. This has naturally led to our growing involvement in corporate governance and a study of the real relationships between directors and management and directors and shareholders. In early 2002 we formed a new company called Board Governance Services, Inc. that works exclusively with boards of directors to assist them in establishing and monitoring the policies, systems, and governance mechanisms required to protect shareholders.

I have no idea what became of the individual executives who sat in that 1981 meeting I described at the beginning of this introduction, but a whole generation of successors has become what those executives disliked. While continuing to produce and distribute real things, they have used their leadership skills not only to manage their employees, but their shareholders as well. They have used financial products, rules-based accounting interpretations, and selective information disclosure to hype their success and mask their failures. They have practiced behavior they previously criticized and justified it because "everyone was doing it." Few did anything illegal, and they have become very rich in the process. Just as some have labeled the past decade as the age of greed, the past quarter century has been the age of financial spin and shading. Although investment bankers, accountants, and securities lawyers ushered in this age, the real momentum was gained when executives became its driving force, using increasingly audacious interpretations of accounting standards and less than exemplary disclosure practices.

A Blueprint for the Future

IN THE PROCESS OF WRITING this book I have talked to many CEOs; directors; strategy, investor relations, and systems consultants; accountants; and investment bankers. Their reactions have tended toward extremes. Many advised me not to write it, arguing that what investors and the public do not know will not hurt them, that the book might further erode confidence, and if nothing else it will make for me a lot of enemies. A few have said that they disagree with its content and conclusions, although that number has declined dramatically as corporate scandals and business failures have continued to unfold. Many others have said that it is about time that this story was told and predicted that the commonsense principles proposed in Chapter 8 will be considered "moderate" in comparison to alternative fixes being suggested as this book goes to print.

Although this book is written primarily from the perspective of investors, it is clearly a plea to executives and directors to honestly reassess the policies, activities, and attitudes they have embraced over time. They need to restore trust in our free market system and in corporations as the organizing entity of this system by supporting real reform, and to reassert their own legitimacy as fiduciaries responsible for putting investors first. Unlike those who support expanding legislation, rule making, and guidelines that strip and curtail the ability of both executives and directors to govern wisely, this book argues that executives and directors must establish a new relationship of common trust and respect.

On March 5, 2003, I had the pleasure of hearing a speech by Lawrence Summers, President of Harvard University. Summers said that Harvard was dedicated to "the authority of ideas instead of the idea of authority." Corporate governance has failed because the idea of authority has overwhelmed the authority of ideas. The conclusion of this book is that embracing the real principles of good governance is ultimately the only way to empower the authority of ideas in corporate America.

SCOTT C. NEWQUIST

CHAPTER 1 # The Crisis in Investor Confidence

NOTHING IN RECENT HISTORY has undermined investor confidence in corporate leaders, governance, and the capital markets more profoundly than the endless stream of stories about corporate failures and misdeeds, disclosure lapses, accounting irregularities, and, in the most disturbing instances, of outright fraud and crime. The unexpected revelations have caused steep declines not only in the prices of the stocks of the companies involved, but also in the market as a whole.

One fact has become all too obvious: the capital markets and individual investors have been gamed. The information needed to assess risk and performance intelligently and to make sound investment decisions has not been made available. Often disclosures were timed to further the interests of the very people charged with protecting the interests of investors—the management.

As a result, many have been hurt. Investment portfolios have been devastated. The savings that many placed in the stock market have been cut in half or more. Investors are reassessing their retirement plans, and those who invested heavily in their employer's stock have seen their pensions shrivel to practically nothing. As companies scramble to maintain earnings growth, tens of thousands of workers have been laid off.

1

The processes designed to ensure that corporations are run to benefit shareholders rather than those in charge of managing the company have failed.

Calls for accountability, reform, and retribution have come from all fronts: investors, legislators, regulators, the press, and the general public. Most of the movement toward reform so far, however, has come in the form of rules and regulations. While these may contribute to the cure, they are generally narrow, shortsighted legislative and regulatory "fixes" that fail to attack the root causes of the problems facing investors and the capital market system—a systematic failure of checks and balances in corporate governance.

The processes designed to ensure that corporations are run to benefit shareholders rather than those in charge of managing the company have failed. A healthy, functioning checks and balances system is the responsibility of boards of directors, who serve as fiduciaries for shareholders. *Fiduciary,* a term used frequently throughout this book, is defined as "holding or held in trust." A crisis of confidence exists now largely because investor trust has been broken by those who held it.

New rules introduced to solve the crisis in governance seem destined to produce less than satisfactory results and will almost surely lead to unintended consequences. The more specifically a rule is constructed, the more creative the ways around it become.

Unless individual corporate executives and directors significantly increase their commitment to principles of good corporate governance and live by those principles day to day, the legislated reforms will lead to more and more ineffective rules and a stalemate with angry investors. Under that scenario, it may become impossible for corporate executives and directors to sustain the highly productive free market system that has been tainted by excesses.

Too Common for Comfort

MOST OF THE PUBLIC and media attention has been focused on high-profile cases of corporate fraud, the ones that resulted in bankruptcy or staggering one-week stock declines. Everyone who has followed the news with even moderate interest can name these companies (Enron, WorldCom, Tyco, Cendant, Adelphia, Global Crossing, Qwest, HealthSouth) and some of their key players. FIGURES 1-1 through 1-5 graphically demonstrate how specific events and the actions of corporate executives trigger significant stock price declines. It has become clear that executives can manipulate stock price over the short run by playing the Share Price Game, the intentional management and manufacture of earnings and manipulation of stock price (more fully described in Chapters 4 and 5). Although individual companies may be cited here as examples of what can go wrong, the purpose is not to fix blame for past lapses, but rather to provide lessons on how to protect the interests of investors going forward.

First labeled as one-off events, the malfeasance is now recognized as much more common than most would have imagined. Even some of the world's leading companies show a willful obfuscation of truth, bending of the rules, and misleading disclosure. Perhaps they've stayed out of big trouble because they have fundamentally sound businesses, capable management teams, or the stature with regulators required to deflect investigations. Or perhaps they simply spin a good enough story to avoid the scandals that have destroyed other companies.

The issues that should be of concern to investors in these companies are not black and white. Instead, they come in many shades of gray. While many practices may not be illegal, they meet the letter of the law through *technicalities* rather than by intent. How often in the recent past have corporate executives explained their behavior by saying that what they did "was not illegal," that it "conformed to GAAP," that they "disclosed what the law required," or that "everyone does it"? Ultimately, investors must

FIGURE 1-1
Cendant (CD) Share Price Time Line

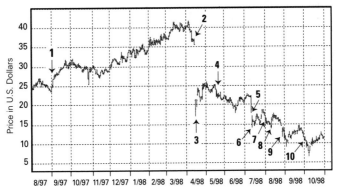

1. HFS, Inc. and CUC International announce plans to merge into new company called Cendant. **2.** Cendant finds accounting irregularities in its former CUC units. Expects to restate earnings for 1997 by $100MM. **3.** Stock loses $14B of market value. **4.** Cendant fires Ernst & Young, former auditors of CUC. **5.** Company announces that earnings for 1995 and 1996 will also need to be restated. **6.** Stock falls 17% on announcement that accounting fraud is more pervasive than first thought. **7.** Walter Forbes, chairman of Cendant (former Chairman/CEO of CUC), is fired. Receives $35MM severance. **8.** Cendant lowers 1997 results by $0.28 per share, 1996 by $0.18 per share, and 1995 by $0.14 per share. **9.** Audit committee delays release of 10-K for 30 days to conduct further review. **10.** Company files restatement of past results.

decide if such explanations are acceptable, because in a capitalist system they are the judges. Unfortunately, they are also the victims when the explanations don't match up well with the truth.

Investors don't get a great deal of credible support. Commentators in the print and broadcast media are routinely congratulatory when only a few weeks or months go by without another blockbuster corporate scandal. At the same time, they report daily on corporate restatements of financial reports, inflated revenue and earnings reports, nondisclosure, obfuscation, or active earnings management. They seldom state the obvious: that what they are reporting on almost always leads to large scandals over time.

Unless individual corporate executives and directors commit to principles of good corporate governance, legislated reforms will lead to more and more ineffective rules.

That such behavior is considered "business as usual" in so many companies is precisely the problem. At what point does spinning the best story by bending or selectively reporting the facts become unacceptable? Many corporate executives, directors, employees, regulators, research analysts, and investors have convinced themselves that these practices ultimately benefit everyone. They argue that shareholder wealth is increased and better management teams can be attracted to companies that bend the rules, leading to a treacherous cycle of earnings misrepresentation, perceived growth, stock price increases, and wealth creation followed by recognition of reality and price collapse.

Investors, faced with huge losses, are beginning to see through this story. They suspect that some of our business leaders are less concerned with increasing shareholder value and wealth than with perpetuating a system that allows a few to profit at the expense of many. No doubt there are investors who succeeded in making and holding on to huge profits over the past five or ten years. All it took was buying in the early 1990s and selling in 1999 or 2000. Most investors who have avoided being burned are those who did not participate in the market at all— not exactly a ringing endorsement of the current system or those who lead it.

The United States is blessed with the most sophisticated and efficient capital markets in the world. Better than any other, they allocate and price equity and debt capital based on information—regarding historical performance, expected future performance, and risks—known and understood by the market.

Control, obfuscation, and manipulation of information by the few are not consistent with capitalism. By shading "historical fact," future expectations are heavily influenced, rendering investors' decisions irrelevant. It's even worse when those who control information do it for their own profit, at the expense of those who depend on them for leadership.

At a time when technology could be providing better and more timely information about increasingly complex businesses, investors may be less accurately informed than ever.

Somewhat ironically, at a time when technology could be providing more, better, and more timely information concerning increasingly complex businesses, investors may be less accurately informed than ever. In small part this is because complexity may have outpaced investors' ability to absorb information. Many businesses believe that "inflating expectations creates wealth, so let's selectively report good news, avoid bad news, and cast everything in the best light."

Certainly many executives and directors work diligently to create investor value, honestly reporting the facts that they believe are relevant and earnestly attempting to fulfill their fiduciary obligations. Most executives and directors would probably place themselves in this group. Undoubtedly, they could all also name peers and acquaintances who might fall into a less favorable category. Members of the public and investors in particular might be less generous still: According to The Conference Board Commission on Public Trust and Private Enterprise, a CNN/USA Today/Gallup poll survey conducted in July 2002 found that about only one-fourth of the respondents feel that most CEOs of large corporations can be trusted.[1]

Is it fair that all executives and directors seem to have been tarred with the same brush of distrust? No, but at the same time, they cannot be held entirely blameless. With leadership comes responsibility. Leaders who have even second-hand knowledge of abuses such as consistently overreporting earnings, hiding lia-

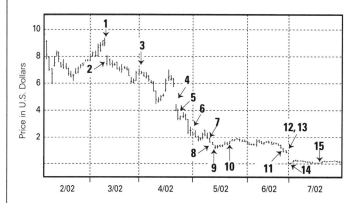

FIGURE 1-2
WorldCom (WCOEQ) Share Price Time Line

1. SEC requests information relating to accounting procedures and loans to officers. 2. Stock falls on news of SEC request. 3. WorldCom cuts 3,700 jobs in the U.S. 4. S&P cuts credit rating on long- and short-term debt. 5. Moody's and Fitch cut credit ratings. 6. President and CEO Bernie Ebbers resigns. John Sidgmore takes over. 7. Moody's cuts WorldCom LT debt rating to junk status. 8. S&P cuts rating on LT debt to junk rating. 9. S&P removes WorldCom from S&P 500. 10. Company announces elimination of dividend and two tracking stocks. 11. WorldCom fires CFO Scott Sullivan after uncovering improper account of $3.8B in expenses. 12. SEC files civil fraud charges against WorldCom. 13. Nasdaq halts trading of stock. 14. Stock resumes trading at $0.07 per share. 15. WorldCom files for Chapter 11 bankruptcy protection. In August, CFO Scott Sullivan and controller David Myers arrested for fraud.

bilities, putting forth only a favorable spin, or failing to disclose real risks have not spoken up. Even individuals of recognized integrity and honesty have by their silence furthered the cause of those who were less forthcoming, manipulative, or plainly dishonest. Abuses have not been the result of one big lie, but rather of many small, relatively inconsequential shadings of the truth that have compounded into much larger offenses.

Management and director insiders had incentives for their deeds: They stood to make a great deal of money. Because the identity of those harmed was not well understood or defined, few felt much guilt. In addition, until abuses became very flagrant, the probability of being caught and the penalties if caught were so low, that it was clearly worth the risk of revealing less than the whole truth. The result: Governance problems are widespread.

Not Without Precedent

THIS ISN'T THE FIRST TIME in history that the public's confidence has been betrayed by corporate executives and business leaders and directors. One need only to open the pages of any American history text to read of the exploits of the late nineteenth-century railroad and industrial robber barons who took advantage of legal loopholes and the lack of regulatory oversight to confound investors and secure their own wealth. The Roaring Twenties ended in the stock market crash of 1929, which wreaked financial ruin on corporations and individuals alike and triggered the Great Depression of the 1930s.

In these historical instances when investor trust has been betrayed, legislators and regulators have intervened, for example, by passing laws to thwart the robber barons of the Gilded Age or by creating regulatory systems to ensure that corporations report their financial performance accurately and fairly. The Securities and Exchange Act of 1934 put into place such a system to protect investors from securities manipulation and fraud. Yet, as history has proven, any set of rules and regulations can be circumvented. The tax code, health care reimbursement, Generally Accepted Accounting Principles (GAAP), and air and water pollution regulations are routinely stretched. Lawmakers often spend months debating and passing new regulations, but it takes bankers and lawyers only a matter of days to find ways to avoid their intent.

Over time, capitalism was adapted to recognize that companies were increasingly owned by a dispersed group of shareholders trading in developed capital markets. Companies were run by professional managers who were not necessarily owners and therefore had different interests than owner/managers of the past. As a result, to protect investor interests, a governance system developed modeled on old English law, based on integrity and trust, and enforced by new laws. The premise was that integrity and judgment were more difficult to finagle than rules, regulations, and laws.

Abuses have not been the result of one big lie, but rather of many small, relatively inconsequential shadings of the truth that have compounded into much larger offenses.

In that system, boards of directors are supposed to represent shareholders' interest as fiduciaries and have oversight responsibility for executive management. Directors are responsible to shareholders. Independent auditors are to provide assurance that reported financial performance is consistent with accepted accounting principles. But directors are responsible for ensuring that investors not only are not misled, but also are given all the information they might need to assess the risk and performance of the companies they own or might own. Directors are proactively monitoring management's actions for investors.

New laws, new regulations, and new checklists of best practices will all be helpful in restoring public trust in the markets. Whether more stringent regulation, stricter enforcement, and harsher penalties can solve the current crisis in investor confidence remains open for debate. One thing is sure: Without dramatic changes in behavior in executive suites and boardrooms of corporations large and small, laws and regulation will exist only to be circumvented and broken again. Shouldn't investors and the public expect that business leaders would police themselves to avoid a repeat performance somewhere down the line?

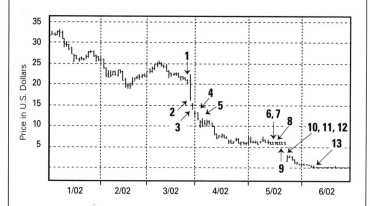

FIGURE 1-3
Adelphia (ADELQ) Share Price Time Line

1. Adelphia discloses that Rigas family has borrowed $2.3B through off-balance sheet family-owned partnerships. **2.** Company acknowledges that it may be liable for additional $5MM in contingent liabilities borrowed by Rigases. **3.** Adelphia delays annual report filing as it needs more time to review financials. **4.** Adelphia says it expects to restate 1999, 2000, and 2001 financial results.**5.** Company announces it is subject of informal SEC inquiry. **6.** Trading of Adelphia stock is halted. **7.** John Rigas announces he is stepping down as chairman. Nasdaq halts trading. **8.** Company announces resignation of CFO Timothy Rigas. **9.** Adelphia misses $44.7MM in bond interest payments. **10.** Trading of stock resumes. **11.** Rigas family relinquishes control as John Rigas and sons Timothy, Michael, and James resign as directors. **12.** Company estimates it is liable for $3.1B in family's debt. **13.** Nasdaq delists company stock, which trades at $0.75 on OTC market. In the summer, Adelphia files for bankruptcy, and in September, a federal grand jury indicts five former executives (including three members of the Rigas family) on charges including conspiracy and securities and wire fraud.

Everyone Wants Someone to Blame

AMONG THE MOST DAMNING criticisms in the current crisis are that corporate leaders (CEOs, CFOs, management teams, and directors) have focused almost exclusively on delivering a smoothly rising stream of quarterly earnings growth at the expense of long-term value creation. They have managed earnings and, when they felt it necessary, manufactured earnings using increasingly more aggressive and far-fetched interpretations of accounting principles. They have avoided transparency through the sheer complexity of modern-day corporations, the selective disclosure of information, and the careful crafting of earnings definitions to control stock prices. They've manipulated pension funds, created partnerships to obscure debt levels and risks, and capitalized operating expenses. And they have used—and abused—stock options to inflate their personal earnings at a great cost to others.

This frenzy of selective disclosure and spin was illustrated by the position taken by William Webster several days prior to his withdrawing as chairman of the Sarbanes-Oxley mandated accounting oversight board. Webster noted that he was a uncompensated director of U.S. Technologies who had worked as hard and diligently as could be expected. He received no salary but stood to gain $890,000 for every $1 rise in stock price.[2] Perhaps it isn't called salary, but few would argue that the opportunity to make such an amount of money as a result of rising stock prices is not compensation.

Who Got Hurt?

THE STORIES OF PERSONAL and collective losses resulting from recent corporate failures have been told many times. But any discussion of the crisis—especially one that proposes recommendations to prevent a similar crisis in the future—must at least recount in summary the widespread devastation.

Investors

Obviously, investors—individual and institutional—suffered enormous financial losses in portfolio value as the markets plunged. As of spring 2003, the Dow Jones Industrial Average had lost almost 37 percent, the Nasdaq about 75 percent, and the S&P 500 about 48 percent since their highs in first quarter 2000. It is difficult to separate the relative market declines attributable to a slowing of the economy, a loss of confidence in reported earnings, a loss of trust in corporate leaders, and a reassessment of historical growth rates that implicitly led investors to expect lower future growth rates. Most CEOs and directors find it less threatening to blame "the economy" than the governance-related causes of a declining market.

Access to the information available didn't serve institutional investors all that well. Many have written off billions in practically valueless stocks and bonds.

Some have argued that losses in real value were not that great because stock market valuations never should have been so high anyway. They say that wealth creation was not real and only temporary in the bubble so that losses were overstated. While this argument may be true in the aggregate, it is certainly not true for each individual who bought heavily in the late 1990s based on unrealistic forecasts of future growth and current earnings. It is cold comfort for investors who, based on paper profits, borrowed heavily to consume, only to see profits disappear rapidly while their debt now remains. This predicament will be exacerbated if interest rates rise as a result of increasing defaults or rising inflation.

Individual investors may have suffered more relative pain than institutional investors because they lack the experience, access to information, and ability to convert information to knowledge leading to the better decision-making capacity of their more sophisticated institutional counterparts. Not that access—at least to the information available—served institutional investors all that well. Many have written off billions in practically valueless stocks and bonds.

Employees

Psychologists say that losing one's job ranks in terms of human trauma with the death of a loved one. This trauma is magnified many times when pension assets, accumulated over many years of labor and thought to be protected, are wiped out by catastrophic governance lapses. More subtle, but perhaps just as devastating for employees retiring in the future, is the systematic underfunding of pension plans resulting from the need to bolster reported earnings. Finally, the loss of employer-paid health insurance has hurt many employees and put pressure on government to provide these entitlements, similar to the situation in Germany and other European countries.

Labor mobility—including movement due to layoffs and even bankruptcies—is a necessary part of the capitalist economic system. It allows labor resources to be shifted to businesses that are growing. Because there is a cost to society of this reallocation process (including lost productivity in transition, disincentives of unemployment insurance, human anguish, and the cost of rehiring employees when growth resumes), many have questioned companies that lay off large numbers of employees, or buy or sell companies only to meet short-term earnings targets. Of the thousands of employees laid off as a result of corporate failures, many have found themselves virtually pensionless and, in many cases, without even basic health care coverage.[3] According to the *New York Times* of June 28, 2002, public pension funds had lost in excess of an estimated $1 billion in WorldCom stock alone and untold billions of dollars more in other beleaguered companies' bonds and stocks.[4]

The same *New York Times* article quotes Tom Herndon, executive director of the Florida State Board of Administration, which lost more than $400 million in WorldCom and Enron stock: "The time is over for the chief executive to sit in his multimillion-dollar mansion in Aspen and laugh at all the shareholders who have lost their life savings. These people ought to be punished, and the institutional investors ought to be one of the parties to take up the cry. "

The Broader Fallout

In a free economy, the abuses or ultimate failure of a few or even one very large enterprise can have many secondary impacts. In economics, this is called the multiplier effect. For example, coordinated efforts by a handful of energy trading companies to inflate their revenue numbers may have contributed to power shortages and high energy prices in California, which in turn may have contributed to bankruptcy or harm to thousands of businesses. Doubtless there are other examples waiting to be discovered. Some have suggested that in the pharmaceutical industry, the time allotted to research and testing may have been shortened to get new drugs to market faster. If this is true, the consequences of focusing on short-term growth may become evident only over the long term.

On Whose Watch Did It Happen?

INVESTORS, OF COURSE, want someone to blame when they lose money. At various times over the year aberrant CEOs, chief financial officers, auditors, research analysts, the New York Stock Exchange, investment banks, and directors have come into the crosshairs, depending on the latest breaking story. In cases like Enron, WorldCom, Adelphia, and Tyco, to name just a very prominent few, there are plenty of culprits to target. But supporters and critics of the equity markets alike would agree that investors are also to blame. They have the responsibility to get to know a company before they invest and to understand that every stock purchase carries with it a certain amount of risk. Shareholders were very happy with their investments in companies as long as stock prices were rising. They did not want to hear, see, or say anything negative or even realistic about their investments until the sheer weight of the lies caused a catastrophic failure.

FIGURE 1-4

Enron (ENRNQ) Share Price Time Line

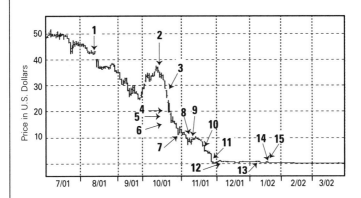

1. Jeff Skilling resigns as CEO after only six months on the job. **2.** Enron reports $618MM Q3 loss and discloses $1.2B in equity related to off-balance sheet partnerships. **3.** SEC sends letter requesting information related to partnerships. **4.** Company acknowledges SEC inquiry into off-balance sheet partnerships. **5.** Ken Lay, now CEO, reassures investors that the worst is behind. **6.** Andrew Fastow, CFO, is fired. **7.** SEC inquiry is upgraded to a formal investigation. **8.** Enron files documents with SEC revising financial statement to account for $586MM in losses. **9.** Company discloses that it overstated earnings by $567MM since 1997. **10.** Enron restates Q3 earnings. **11.** Credit rating is cut to junk status by all rating agencies. **12.** Company files for Chapter 11 bankruptcy protection. **13.** Criminal investigation is begun by Justice Department. **14.** Former employee claims she saw documents being shredded after announcement of SEC investigation. **15.** Ken Lay resigns as CEO. Later that fall, former CFO Andrew Fastow pleads not guilty to charges of securities, wire and mail fraud; money laundering; and conspiracy.

But blaming investors for all of their woes smacks of blaming the victim for the crime. Assume that investors—and all the others who suffered for that matter—had done exemplary due diligence and then had used all the information to which they had access. Would they have made different investment decisions? Would they have been able to influence change in the companies before it was too late? Would they have had a meaningful voice in approving or disapproving the decisions that ultimately led to catastrophe? Most likely not. Investors rely on information reported by companies and assured by independent auditors. They depend on research reports and recommendations from supposedly independent research analysts to convert masses of complex information to knowledge. They feel that laws and regulations will protect them from lies, fraud, and unbridled corporate greed. Most of all, as shareholders, they trust that corporate management will fulfill its responsibilities to create value and that boards will represent and protect their interest.

The Loss of Legitimacy

Companies, CEOs, directors, auditing firms, analysts, and investment bankers have all suffered from a loss of reputation and legitimacy. Confidence in these individuals and institutions is very low. Witness the number of antibusiness articles and media commentary, the negative findings of public opinion polls such as the report of The Conference Board mentioned previously, and the dramatic increases in restatements of financial statements within the past few years. The assessments of the situation and responses of the individuals and institutions that are now held in low regard varies tremendously and generally fall into three categories.

In the first category, many executives and directors simply continue to ignore the issue or simply hope that it will go away. Either they are in a state of denial or are so self-absorbed that they believe meaningful criticism of them is unthinkable. To the extent that they recognize that confidence in them has been lost, they assume it will be restored as soon as the markets recover. Some have simply not accepted that they are largely responsible for both the market bubble and decline and even view themselves as among the victims.

A second group recognizes the loss of confidence but believes that by saying "it just ain't so" it will be restored. Members of this group routinely declare that governance problems have been solved. As evidence, they point to their compliance with good governance checklists. They blame poor stock market performance on something other

In a free economy, the abuses of a few very large enterprises can have many secondary impacts. In economics, this is called the multiplier effect.

than governance and keep talking up stock prices by spinning growth stories, manufacturing earnings, and downplaying risks.

Yet a third group believes that the market may not recover substantially for an extended period or until real reform and fundamental change occur. In this scenario, the restoration of confidence has to precede a real recovery. The authors of this book fall into this category.

The current crisis in confidence differs from the many that preceded it. In previous crises, investors lost faith in executives' and directors' judgment and their ability to adapt strategies that would make their companies successful, like those who saw the dominant companies in the 1970s and 1980s disappear. While investors questioned the understanding and judgment of their fiduciaries, there is no ethical, moral, or legal requirement that fiduciaries must be right; they are only obligated to try to be so. In contrast, in the current crisis, investors believe that they were lied to and purposely misled.

In short, the legitimacy of corporations, executives, boards of directors, Wall Street bankers and analysts, accountants, institutional money managers, and many participants in the economic system is being questioned. Federal legislation has mandated a new oversight board for the accounting profession. Proposals have been made to establish an oversight body for mutual funds. Major stock exchanges and other regulatory bodies are dictating board committee structures, profiles of directors, new reporting requirements, the number of required board meetings, and who may

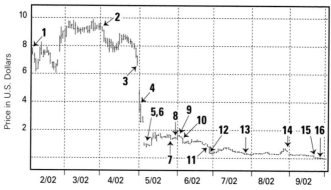

FIGURE 1-5
Peregrine (PRGNQ) Share Price Time Line

1. Chris Cole, director of Peregrine, begins selling 500,000 shares over next 9 days.
2. Company fires auditor Arthur Andersen and hires KPMG. **3.** Peregrine announces
it will delay earnings report to allow KPMG more time to review books. **4.** Shares fall
50% to $3.45 on announcement of delay in filing quarterly earnings report.
5. Company announces it has launched internal investigation and may need to restate
up to $100MM. **6.** CEO and CFO resign. **7.** SEC opens investigation. **8.** Company
announces that it has fired KPMG as auditor. **9.** Gary Greenfield hired as CEO. Rod
Dammeyer resigns from board. Eric Deller, general council, resigns. **10.** KPMG
announces it was fired for uncovering accounting fraud beyond original scope.
11. Peregrine hires PricewaterhouseCoopers as new auditors. **12.** Nasdaq
announces it will delist Peregrine the following month due to listing violations.
13. Bondholders express concerns over financial affairs. **14.** Company announces
plans to restate reported revenue by $250MM or 19% of sales and $103MM in additional debt. **15.** It files for Chapter 11 bankruptcy protection. **16.** U.S. Justice
Department launches criminal investigation into accounting issues.

CHART: BLOOMBERG L.P.

attend, while some are facing increasing public criticism of their
own governance practices. Investment bankers and analysts have
been attacked, and independent research has been mandated—

although ineffectively at the date of this writing. Trade unions have attacked corporate governance and ethics and have demanded transparency, even while remaining virtually opaque themselves and diverting large portions of membership dues to their leaders. Finger pointing is rampant.

The implications of this cannot be understated. Simple loss of confidence in the judgments of leaders can be fixed by recognizing new winners and leaders. Lost legitimacy requires real changes to the system. The longer it takes to adopt and follow governance principles that benefit everyone, the more drastic those changes must be. The principles outlined in Chapter 8 can help reinforce, reinvigorate, and legitimize the system that everyone once thought was working so well.

In the absence of changes like those proposed in Chapter 8, a new system may have to be created. Unless boards of directors and executives take meaningful actions to address past lapses and go beyond lip service, something else will replace their offices and positions. Those mechanisms will likely be legally mandated, with power shifted to more centralized authority and arguably more subject to political pressures that are often more emotional than reasoned.

This legalistic path is not one that many want to take, but vacuums of responsibility are always filled. Even worse, unless accountability changes in the capital markets, there could be a real loss of legitimacy for democracy and the United States. Free markets and democracy can exist independently, but they are closely linked in the world's perception of the United States. Because of a committed work force and sophisticated markets, America has succeeded in delivering relatively sustained growth. Through a dynamic political system, the country has extended economic success to a great majority of all productive workers. There is little doubt that the United States has done a better job of creating financial well being for its citizens than most countries. That success, however, has fostered dislike or even contempt in other parts of the world, even among U.S. allies in Europe.

The principles of good governance discussed in Chapter 8, if adopted and followed, will work to help restore legitimacy and confidence.

Over the past decade or two, America has encouraged both democracy and free market initiatives, including privatization and entrepreneurship, in Asia, the Middle East, and parts of Africa. Growth in those economies accelerated as a result. We may have been less successful at introducing the checks and balances required to ensure that the benefits of a free market economy reach a substantial proportion of the population. In some instances wealth has become concentrated in very few hands and many around the world may indirectly blame America for an increase in their relative poverty.[5]

Against this backdrop, the United States simply cannot ignore even a hint of a loss of legitimacy. The risks are too high. The misconceptions and misalignment of interests discussed in the next chapter are not harmless. The abuses of options explained in Chapter 3 contributed significantly to the loss of confidence. Playing the Share Price Game (Chapters 4 and 5) had sobering consequences. The paucity of corporate checks and balances covered in Chapter 6 permitted abuses involving income distribution, market inefficiency, poor capital and labor allocation, and bankruptcy. Chapter 7 lays out the need for more independent, effective, and informed boards, the fundamental requirement of good governance. In the absence of better boards, the U.S. economic system is threatened. The principles of good governance discussed in Chapter 8, if adopted and followed, will work to help restore legitimacy and confidence.

Investors should insist on real reform. They cannot fully trust again until their trust has been earned and mechanisms put in place to verify that such trust is deserved.

CHAPTER 2 # The Alignment of Interests

THERE WAS A TIME when companies were both owned and managed by the same people, often by generation after generation of a single family. These owners/managers typically took a long-term view of how well their companies performed. Not only did they expect to own and manage their businesses for their entire working lives, they also expected to leave their businesses to their children, who would then assume the owner/manager role and responsibilities. The motives, interests, and actions of the owners/managers all aligned with the long-term success of the company and concentrated on building enduring, intrinsic value. That value came from sustaining the business as a competitive enterprise that would generate cash over many years.

As companies grew and economies shifted, the dynamics of the owner/manager model changed dramatically. For many different reasons, ranging from the difficulties of managing increasingly complex businesses to simply a lack of interest by successive generations, companies began to hire professional managers. This created a distinct separation between the owners and management, which in turn created what is called the "agency" issue. With the owners no longer intimately involved in day-to-day business operations, they needed to ensure that the professional managers they hired—their agents—ran things for the benefit of both the owners and the enterprise as a whole. Boards of directors were created to serve this oversight function and to provide a system of checks and balances to ensure that management not only performed ethically and honestly but also focused on building long-term value for the owners.

The advent of the capital markets also dramatically changed the owner/manager model. Selling shares of stock in a company provided a way to attract money from investors who were neither the dynastic owners nor the professional managers. When "outsiders" began to share in the company's ownership, their separation from managers became even more distinct and distant, requiring a more robust system of checks and balances to monitor the agency problem.

Over time, the combination of the agency issue and the dispersion of ownership created two major governance paradoxes for publicly traded companies:

- **Shareholder identity is often misdefined.** In today's volatile market, the majority of shareholders are short-term investors, more interested in changes in share price than in long-term value creation. But higher share price is in the interest of all shareholders only when the increase is permanent and based on real earnings and sustainable growth. To fulfill their fiduciary responsibilities to all shareholders (past, present, and future), directors must take a longer-term view because only when stock price truly reflects real value do all shareholders, regardless of when they buy or sell their shares, benefit over time.

- **The ability of investors to trade shares at will, moment by moment, puts individual shareholders in competition with each other.** Only long-term growth in real enterprise value aligns the interests of shareholders. When shareholders compete as traders in the equity markets, their interests are nonaligned. This competition—the desire to buy low and to sell high—has inherently misaligned shareholders' individual interests in the short term. When corporate executives and directors, who have inside information, buy and sell their shares with other investors, the misalignment becomes a grave governance issue.

Paradox 1:
The Shareholder Identity Crises

IN A PRIVATELY HELD COMPANY where ownership does not change except by passing from generation to generation, the identity of the shareholders is obvious. Yesterday's shareholders, today's shareholders, and tomorrow's shareholders stay the same. In a modern corporation where millions of shares trade daily, and the specific identity of the shareholders changes by the minute, ownership is dynamic. The tendency is still to think of shareholders as a static group with fairly well-aligned investment goals and financial interests because of their ownership in the company.

That concept makes sense only in a very few instances, however, such as determining who receives a dividend, who can attend annual meetings, or who has standing in certain lawsuits. In most other contexts, it makes much better sense to define shareholders as not only those who own stock now, but also those who might buy stock in the future and those who have owned shares in the past. The law, in fact, clearly recognizes that except in a few instances like those cited earlier, shareholders include past, current, and future owners of stock.

It's especially logical to include all three groups when considering the obligations of management and directors to provide information on the performance and condition of the business. If a company exaggerates reported earnings or downplays liabilities at any point in time, and these actions are not fully and accurately disclosed, future shareholders will be penalized at the expense of past shareholders. The same argument holds true for current shareholders who bought shares based on incomplete or inaccurate information.

A current shareholder could think, "Who cares about future shareholders? If earnings are overstated, or if liabilities are understated, and the price of my stock goes up today, I'm all in favor. The hell with future shareholders—it's their problem!" This all-too-human perspective is logical in isolation. It is fatally flawed from the perspective of the shareholders' fiduciaries and in the context of free-market capital allocation. First, it assumes that current shareholders will not be future shareholders, and it implies that the shareholders in question decided to sell their stock at or near the top price. Second, this perspective assumes that these shareholders will never buy shares at a price that has been inflated. Unfortunately for most shareholders, these two assumptions seldom hold true consistently.

Because shareholders buy and sell securities based, by definition, on imperfect financial and other information, the definition of ownership has to include all shareholders over time. If shareholders were defined as only those who own stock at a given moment, then any action or nonaction that increased share price temporarily would be justified. But the consequences of adopting this point of view would be dire. Capital would be allocated poorly on a risk-adjusted basis (since investors would not be able to fairly judge the risk or the possible reward of inflated stocks), and the entire free-market system could not work.

Real Value: The Fiduciary's Objective

As fiduciaries for a company's shareholders, the directors' goal must be increasing the real enterprise value of the company over time. This objective alone aligns the interests of all shareholders, and it differs markedly from an interest in pushing share price to the highest possible level. When fiduciaries allow share price to be inflated above real value, they put the interests of existing shareholders ahead of the interests of future shareholders.

The job of management is not to persuade investors that share price will rise continuously—unless, of course, true value increases as well. Management certainly should not set out to provide inaccurate or misleading information. Only when management focuses on creating long-term value and when executives and directors ensure that complete and accurate information regarding both risks and rewards is communicated without bias will the collective wisdom of investors set share price at or near its real value. The responsibility for providing complete, accurate, and timely information lies not only with corporate executives, management teams, and boards of directors, but also with research analysts and other corporate advisers such as independent auditors, lawyers, and investment bankers. And all must consider current, past, and future shareholders when fulfilling their duties and responsibilities.

Enron's management and board were perceived to have performed well for investors when, based on false earnings, the stock rose from approximately $20 to $90 in less than

> *To fulfill their fiduciary responsibilities to all shareholders, directors must take a longer-term view. Only when stock price truly reflects real value do all shareholders benefit over time.*

two years ending in the summer of 2000. When the price approached zero, shareholders had a very different perception.

Confusion Over Shareholder Identity

What makes the capital allocation system work well is the ability of an individual investor to do a better analysis of the prospects of a company and to have the patience, courage of conviction, and wisdom to buy and sell based on that knowledge. This is the measure of the investor's success.

Successful fiduciaries, however, should not be judged on profit or loss records of one investor or a selected group of investors. Fiduciaries should be measured first on the collective performance of all shareholders—past, present, and future—which, over time, will correlate closely to long-term real growth. Their success should also be judged on how well they provide equal and timely access to complete information that allows investors to price securities as closely as possible to real value. Because investors bring emotions to their decisions, prices are sometimes above real value and sometimes below—possibly for extended periods of time. But share price always returns to real value regardless of a fiduciary's performance.

The Tyranny of the Time Frame

That management may have different priorities or objectives from owners is acknowledged. What is less well understood is that these different considerations stem from the fact that management's time horizon is far shorter than shareholders'. Certainly some CEOS and management teams serve for fifteen years or more. Others might argue that they expect to serve for that many or more years, which would lengthen their time frame perspective. This argument is certainly plausible, but the fact remains that as a CEO reaches retirement age, his or her time frame will certainly become shorter.

Not surprisingly, CEOs tend to earn at a much higher rate in the last five years of their tenure. All components of compensation usually rise during this time including salary, bonus, and, most important, their proceeds from cashing in options. It makes sense for CEOs who have accumulated stock options over an extended career to cash them in near retirement. What investors should recognize is that such accumulated options give CEOs a tremendous incentive to maintain growth in the last years of their tenure and even to move earnings into current quarters at the expense of future quarters. Both the risk of falling or flattening growth rates and the reward from sustained or accelerating growth is magnified near the end of a CEO's tenure.

A related part of the time frame problem is that in many instances, new CEOs decide to take a large write-off at the beginning of their tenure. It has been suggested that these write-offs are to establish reserves to allow the new CEO to show growth relatively quickly. It is also likely that write-offs are required to compensate for accelerated earnings that have robbed future periods of the ability to show stable earnings. Whichever it is, shareholders are harmed, and the existing CEO arguably takes home more compensation than earned or anticipated for actual performance achieved.

Because executives are usually shareholders themselves and can control so much of the information a company reports about its financial performance, many have consistently focused on achieving short-term gains to raise the share price at the expense of creating long-term value. Management and CEOs control operations and make daily trade-offs between earnings now or earnings later. They decide how to account for revenue and earnings. It is critical, therefore, that management acts to maximize the long-term value of companies and avoids practices that increase risk without the knowledge of owners.

Fiduciaries should be measured on the collective performance of all shareholders— past, present, and future— which, over time, will correlate closely to long-term real growth.

CEOs seem compelled to operate with two realities. On the one hand, in light of accounting shenanigans (and an extended period of defense spin about their inflated stocks) by the executives at Enron, WorldCom, Adelphia, and the like, there's a renewed belief that CEOs should run their businesses well and let the markets determine what the stock price should be. On the other hand, because of myriad factors including stock-based compensation packages and the fact that share price has become the primary indicator of corporate health and strength, CEOs, investors, the daily press, and Wall Street remain fixed on stock prices. Harvey J. Goldschmid, now an SEC commissioner, reflected on that in an article in the February 18, 2002, issue of *Fortune* magazine, saying, "Previously the CEO's job was much more secure. Today, with CEOs that much more accountable for their stocks' performance, they're under greater pressure to keep the share price up." Keeping share price up certainly benefits short-term investors looking to get out at the top. If that is the only group of shareholders that a CEO is serving, it's definitely time for that CEO to rethink or relearn the true identity of shareholders—past, present, and future.

Directors have also operated at times with a confused notion of shareholder identity. No one disputes that a company's board has the responsibility to protect the shareholders' interests by

assisting in building value and identifying risks. Undoubtedly
many directors make decisions based on long-term value creation
that will benefit all shareholders over time. Like executives, however, directors have too often
viewed their fiduciary obligation as being limited to current
or short-term shareholders. It's
tempting. Gratification is more
immediate, more personal,
and often consistent with self-
interest when the director has
received options or stock as
compensation.

*Managers' success
should be judged on how
well they provide equal
and timely access to
complete information that
allows investors to price
securities as closely as
possible to real value.*

Directors have justified, at
least to themselves, that any action the company may take to
increase stock price benefits shareholders. Many have forgotten
that allowing the stock to be hyped will benefit existing shareholders in the short term, but is quite likely to hurt them in the
long term, and certainly will harm future shareholders who will
buy at inflated, hyped levels.

Although this discussion is really about corporate governance
and fiduciary responsibilities to all shareholders, another
group—research analysts—has consistently failed to take all
shareholders into consideration. This doesn't make sense considering that the customers for their research reports are investors
thinking of both buying and selling shares, which inherently
broadens the definition.

Research analysts have two legitimate roles. The traditional
role is to collect information from the company and elsewhere
and to distill that information for others making investment decisions. The second is to provide visibility for companies so that
investors know to consider a company as a possible investment.
Fulfilling both roles responsibly requires an impartial, independent view of actual earnings, historical growth rates (that are a
proxy for future growth rates), and financial and business risks.
Too often research analysts have issued excessively favorable

research, justifying it in the belief that shareholders will benefit as stock prices rise in the short term.

This shortening of the analyst's view of value is apparent in how research has changed over time. In the old days, it focused on fundamental earning power and included analysis of competitive advantage, value drivers, business risks from changing technology, and financial risks. Now research emphasizes quarterly earnings versus whisper numbers versus last year's performance and so on. It tends to underestimate or ignore unknowns in the future because the focus is so short term.

Paradox 2:
Individual Investors' Competing Interests

ALTHOUGH CORPORATE EXECUTIVES and directors should view shareholders as past, current, and future and behave accordingly, that does not mean individual investors should not act in their own self interest. Investors can buy and sell shares at will and those shares are valued and revalued constantly. In this context, the motivation and interests of buyers and sellers, when viewed singly, are completely unaligned. They compete.

Most often, an investor's objective in owning a stock is to buy low and sell high, and possibly to collect dividends in the interim. This is difficult to do, and risky. Even if the performance and condition of a company continue to improve, the stock price may decline based on poor expectations of future performance. This happens because stock prices are determined by an unknown and uncertain expectations of future events, and because the actual performance, prospects, and risks of companies change constantly. The collective judgment of all investors about these changes creates relative supply and demand for shares and sets their prices, although sometimes market price will vary substantially from real value. Over time, though, market price will return to real value.

Stock prices of individual companies (and the levels of indices representing specific industries and entire markets) do not move in a straight line. When one investor buys low, another investor sells low; when one sells high, another investor buys high. This competition keeps markets efficient and allocates capital to optimize risk and return. Because stocks move up and down, and because each buyer has a corresponding seller and vice versa, investing is sometimes considered a contest of who gets it right. The only way that everyone can get it right is over the long-term as the totality of all stock prices rises.

Keeping share price up certainly benefits short-term investors looking to get out at the top. But that isn't an inclusive definition of shareholders past, present, and future.

Yet because individual investors may have different time frames, it does not follow that when a seller sells and a buyer buys that one is wrong and one is right from the perspective of realized gains and losses. Both can be right or both wrong if they have a different time frame. The end result is a function of the buy price and the sell price.

If investors "knew" with certainty that the stock they own would go up steadily and consistently, they would sell it only if they could identify another stock that they "knew" would go up faster. What investors see is that stocks fluctuate. They also make buy and sell decisions based on fear and greed.

When Executives and Directors Compete as Shareholders

Investors try to time momentum, gain access to information unknown to most other investors, or analyze existing information more intelligently than others. Of course, when one group of investors has inside knowledge not available to others, this competition takes place on a less than level playing field.

When corporate executives and directors are themselves shareholders or holders of stock options, they compete with other shareholders when buying and selling, and they *always* have information unknown and unavailable to other investors. If executives are managing perceptions of earnings, they know the real earnings number. If they are manufacturing earnings, they know the level to which earnings and growth have been over-stated and how much longer they can sustain the inflated num-bers. If they are hiding liabilities or pursuing risky and unsus-tainable business practices, they have a clearer, more complete picture of real risks.

Finally, if management and directors are contemplating com-petitive moves that legitimately cannot be disclosed to investors without sacrificing competitive advantage, they can make a more informed judgment regarding the probability of future events than outside shareholders. CEOs often justify their lack of trans-parency because of the need to sustain competitive advantage. They raise a legitimate issue. It is difficult to understand, how-ever, how they can justify their lack of disclosure and at the same time claim that they do not have inside information.

Executives who claim they don't have information that investors might use cannot, by definition, be doing a good job of managing. (Executives who hide liabilities and risks to manipu-late earnings and stock price have done worse, of course.) The problem becomes even greater when executives or directors compete with others as individual shareholders when buying and selling their stock and use their privileged positions to line their own pockets at the great expense of other shareholders.

Fortune magazine, in collaboration with Thomson Financial and the University of Chicago's Center for Research in Securities Pricing, conducted a study to see how America's top executives behaved as individual shareholders during the post-Enron mar-ket crash. Their findings were reported in an article by Mark Gimein in the August 11, 2002, issue of *Fortune* titled, "The Greedy Bunch: You Bought. They Sold." According to that report, while investors were losing the major portion, or even all, of their holdings, "top officials of many of the companies that have crashed the hardest were getting immensely, extraordinar-ily, obscenely wealthy" by selling their stock, much of it acquired through options, at very inflated prices.

How wealthy did these individuals get? The study focused on

companies that had hit a market cap of at least $400 million and
then had fallen by at least 75 percent and met a few other narrow
criteria. Of the 1,035 companies included, the researchers estimate that executives and directors in those companies cashed in
for approximately $66 billion. The report also notes, "A total haul
of $23 billion went to 466 insiders at the twenty-five corporations
that cashed out the most." Those companies included the very
prominent such as Cisco and AOL Time Warner, and the not so
prominent like Ariba, InfoSpace, and Peregrine Systems.
Topping *Fortune's* list was Qwest Communications, where executives took out $2.26 billion. Phil Anschutz, then chairman, got
almost $1.6 billion.

The article concludes with a quote from Michael Ramsay,
chairman and CEO of TiVo, "It all comes down to your personal
set of rules about what being an executive of a company really
means." Executives aren't "just shareholders like any other shareholders," he says.

The Problems With Equity Compensation

OVER THE PAST DECADE, directors, CEOs, senior managers,
governance experts, and compensation consultants have
preached that by giving directors and management equity stakes
in the business, their interests are aligned with those of the
shareholders. The implied promise has been that by linking
interests through equity ownership, the agency issue—the need
to ensure that management acts in the interests of shareholders
instead of self-interest—is solved and that enhanced shareholder
value will result.

This widely held premise deserves closer inspection, but not
because today's CEOs, directors, and managers are necessarily
overpaid. (In fact, many directors are underpaid for the responsibilities they shoulder, and those CEOs and managers who build
real long-term value for shareholders should be paid handsomely
for their efforts.) The reason to review this logic is to ensure that
the equity component is structured intelligently and that those

who receive it exercise it appropriately. Because stock price can
be so easily massaged by executives, as described in Chapters 3
and 4, and because they can
time their stock purchases and
sales to coincide with lows and
highs in their shares, the equity
portion of compensation should
be carefully crafted and con-

When executives and directors have stock options, they compete with other shareholders when buying and selling, and they always have information unavailable to other investors.

stantly monitored. And, in fact, while equity compensation in the
form of stock options can be appropriate as an incentive to build
real value, many other types of incentives may be more appropriate for better aligning management's interests with those of the
shareholders.

The Roots of the Equity Compensation Model

The leveraged buyout (LBO) movement of the 1980s provided
the model and justification for public companies to compensate
both management and directors in equity-based securities, primarily options. As management teams of LBOs profited handsomely from their "equity" in the form of a carried interest in
profits, other CEOs from some large, established companies
argued for and received large option grants so they too could
enjoy the same kind of upside. Soon, still more corporate executives joined in the bonanza, uniformly supporting options and
other forms of equity as the major component of compensation.

The flaw in their logic is that an LBO results in a private company, a very different entity from a public company. The stock is
not traded, and value is generally created as expenses are slashed
and cash flow pays down debt. Management and owners make
money by maximizing cash flow and, if anything, minimizing
earnings to reduce taxes (already reduced by high debt levels and
the associated interest expense). As this process unfolds, no
shareholder sells while others hold or buy. All shareholders benefit from retiring debt. What they can do is time everyone's exit,

or partial exit, by selling in one transaction or through an initial public offering (IPO). Unless the company is sold to another LBO group and releveraged, the exit generally converts the private company back to public ownership, either as a stand-alone company or as part of an existing public one. When this occurs, the new company creates value for shareholders not by paying down debt, but by growing earnings and cash flow, which ultimately will benefit shareholders.

The leveraged buy-out movement of the 1980s provided the model and justification for public companies to compensate both management and directors in equity.

The LBO precedent set in the 1980s also prompted directors of public companies to endorse equity compensation for themselves. In 1995 the Committee on Director Compensation of the National Association of Corporate Directors recommended abolishing obvious conflicts such as lavish benefit plans, providing other services for compensation, and, for the first time, requiring full disclosure of compensation for directors. At the same time, the Committee also recommended that options or other stock-based compensation be the primary source of director pay.

When options for both management and directors became widely adopted, many heralded it as a radical reformation of corporate oversight. That it was, but not to the benefit of investors. Paying directors in equity, or in options that could be cashed in on a regular basis, cemented the interests of directors with those of management, tightly binding their personal interests to relatively short-term stock price performance. Forgotten or ignored was the lesson of the LBO era—that aligning interests required not only participation in upside but also in downside risk. Ignored were the differences between private and pubic companies.

As things turned out, these differences were not just theoretical. Widespread earnings and stock price management, earnings manufacture, and the gaming of options have focused management's attention on these practices rather than on managing the company to create long-term value. And directors, rather than acting as a check against these tendencies, now have parallel interests with management rather than with shareholders.

Are All Options Programs Bad for Investors?

The next chapter, "How Options Work," offers a more in-depth discussion of executive and employee stock options, including how they work, who gets them, and why. Because so many employees and executives have made so much money from options—often just before investors learned that inflated stock prices did not reflect real value—this discussion is understandably a contentious one. It is nonetheless important in gaining a better understanding of how shareholders' interests may not always take precedence.

Boards that use options to compensate executives who have the ability to manipulate earnings are asking for trouble. This is not to say that boards should never use options as a component of executive compensation, but it certainly does place an added burden on directors to monitor executives' behavior. Former SEC Chairman Harvey Pitt summed up the options-for-executives quandary succinctly, "If managers can reap profits from their options while shareholders are losing some or all of their equity stake, the options create conflicting, not aligned interests."[1] Certainly, when options are extended to those in control of the numbers, they should be structured in a way that requires the recipient to hold them long beyond a time when they can willfully manage stock price.

Granting options to nonexecutive employees is more easily justified. This group cannot directly manipulate stock price, so the risk of creating bad behavior is minimal. One would certainly expect employees to contribute more to the company and to care about its real performance if part of their compensation is in the form of a long-term equity interest. Many employees, in fact, have such an interest through their 401(k) or pension plans. At the same time, because of external events or internal company issues entirely out of their control, employees can perform exceptionally well and still not profit from options. This alone can mitigate the level of incentive that options provide. Would it not make as much or more sense to reward employees through incentives related to behavior and performance measures?

Who Changed the Rules?

How did executives come to behave as if their primary responsibility was to manage stock price? Why have boards consistently rewarded them for doing so? One interpretation could be that it was an honest mistake. In this charitable view, the executives and directors truly believed that increasing the price of the stock, regardless of how much real value had been created, benefited all shareholders.

But many executives have behaved like competitive individual shareholders, selling their stock high and rationalizing that behavior by asserting, "If it's good for me, it must be good for everyone else." In reality, the good only accrued to those who got out at the top. And who had the best shot at that? The executive insiders who knew how much the share price stood over its real value, and could initiate their sell decisions in advance of the inevitable and precipitous decline, usually won.

A more cynical explanation of this behavior would be that some executives created the system deliberately, and many others came to view it as "business as usual." They knew they could boost share price and then profit personally by doing so. They had opportunity. And despite headlines of a few CEOs having charges pressed against them for egregious corruption, in the broadly played game of hyping their stock prices, they knew there was little risk of getting caught, and even less chance of being prosecuted.

Whether one takes the more charitable view or the more cynical, one thing is certain: By ignoring the well-being of those who would buy high when current shareholders (executives and directors included) sold near or at the top, many executives failed to protect the interests of all shareholders.

That is why the system of equity compensation in the form of stock options raises such a serious corporate governance issue. Options not only fail to resolve the agency problem, but also exacerbate it if executives can freely trade that equity. Not all managers and CEOs who receive large option grants are manipulating the books. But investors in those companies that issue significant options to the CEO and other senior executives should certainly consider it a cause for caution. They should also expect directors on the boards of those companies to pay close attention to the behavior of executives and measure management's performance in building true value in the company and not just on increasing its share price.

CHAPTER 3 # How Options Work

Stock options have been called both the best and worst compensation tool ever devised. The truth can fall at the extremes or anywhere in between, depending on who receives options, why they are issued, and the details of how they are structured. To pass judgment on a single options program or individual grant, one must understand the "who," "why," and "how" of the options in question. Their appropriateness also depends on how closely the behavior of the recipients can be monitored and on the mechanisms available to halt counterproductive behavior (and to reinforce productive behavior). As experience has shown, the absence of stringent monitoring of options can be dangerous indeed for outside investors. In the worst case, senior executives with significant stock options may be motivated to manipulate stock price for their own gain. Any big stock options award has the potential to dilute all other investors, the actual providers of capital.

In simplified terms, when a company awards stock options to an individual, it gives that person the option, or right, to purchase a specified number of shares in the company at some specified time in the future. The price at which the recipient can purchase the stock is called the *strike price,* which is set at the time the option is granted and is usually the stock's current price. Options holders profit when they can exercise their options and sell the resulting stock for more than the strike price. When options are granted to employees instead of stock, the ultimate value to the employee depends not on the value of a share, but on the *increase* in the value of a share, requiring growth—actually, growth in share price. The estimated value of the option reported in the proxy statement is not the value received, but only an estimate based on historical price performance and other factors.

Two control factors are the window of time during which the option can be exercised and turned into stock and the restrictions on when the recipient can sell the resulting stock. For example, the recipient might be allowed to exercise the option within a year but prevented from selling the stock for three or more years from the date the option was issued. In some instances companies will buy the option directly from the holder. When this happens, the holder never has to put up any cash to exercise the option. The exercise and sale are, in effect, simultaneous, which means that no shares are actually issued.

All Options Transfer
Economic Return to Employees

BEFORE CONSIDERING the appropriateness of a specific company's option grants or programs, it is important to understand that all employee options have one thing in common. If the option ends up having value, it transfers ownership and therefore economic return away from the providers of capital—the investors—to the providers of labor—the employees, who themselves may or may not at the time be owners.

When employees exercise options, all existing shareholders are diluted and the intrinsic value of each share of stock they hold is reduced. Employees own a larger proportion of the company and have a larger claim on the future earnings and value of the company. Nonemployee investors, therefore, have a declining right to the profits of the business.

To understand the diluting impact of paying employees in

stock, consider a very simplified example. Assume that in Year 1 XYZ Company is owned entirely by investors, and that there are 100 shares outstanding. Because investors own 100 percent of the company, they have a claim on 100 percent of the earnings, regardless of whether or not they are reinvested. Now, assume that at the start of Year 2, the management of the company gives itself a reward for a job well done in the form of stock equal to 15 percent of the initial outstanding shares. The number of outstanding shares is now 115, with outside investors owning only 87 percent of the company, and management owning 13 percent. The outside investors' stake in the company has been diluted.

When employees exercise options, all existing shareholders are diluted and the intrinsic value of each share of stock they hold is reduced.

This only tackles the issue of ownership dilution. There is also the issue of earnings dilution. Continuing the same example, assume that the company made $100 dollars in profit in Year 1, all of which was paid-out to shareholders in the form of a dividend. Shareholders, therefore, received $1 for every share they owned. Now assume that earnings in Year 2 were also $100. Because of the executive stock grant, the company now has 115 shares outstanding, and assuming that the company continues to pay all of its profits out in the form of dividends, shareholders will receive only eighty-seven cents for each share of stock they own. It is easy to see how issuing additional shares dilutes the profits paid to investors. Management has essentially transferred thirteen cents worth of investors' earnings to itself. The impact of issuing stock, however, is clear from the investor's perspective: a declining proportion of the earnings pie for the investor who contributed the capital and an increasing proportion for those who manage the company.

Investors should understand that if a company issues significant stock options to employees (not offset by stock buybacks), it signals that the investors' return will be limited because profits will be diluted. While investors may not like this, they can adjust the

P/E of the company's stock downward and pay less for the shares they buy, or not buy shares at all. The mathematics is pretty straightforward. When deciding what P/E the company should trade at, the reported historical growth rate of earnings should be reduced by the historical dilution that results when options are exercised. For example, if a company averages 5 percent dilution annually because options are exercised and the company is reporting 11 percent growth, only 6 percent of that growth will benefit investors. Therefore the P/E should be based on 6 percent growth and not 11 percent.

Is it wrong for companies to transfer profits away from investors and give them to labor in the form of stock? Certainly not. In some industries, especially technology, health care, and others where education and highly developed knowledge and skills are critical to success, returning more of the company's profits to labor and less to investors may be appropriate. If it is the policy of the company to do so, then that policy should be explicit and fully disclosed. Many companies do, in fact, report in detail to investors that labor receives large stock or option incentives. With full disclosure and understanding, investors can make informed decisions.

Assessing the
Appropriateness of Options

IF JUDGING OPTIONS depends on the "who," "why," and "how," investors should look carefully at each question.

Who Receives Options?
Most recipients fall into two groups. The first is senior executives, who have the ability to influence reported profits and disclosed risks and who make important business decisions that affect company practices and methods of doing business. Giving options to senior executives can materially change their behavior. For example, they may inflate profits or downplay or not disclose risks Because their options only give them the upside and no downside

risk, they may be inclined to take inappropriate risks, knowing that even if stock price declines they can also get more options at a lower price with the potential for cashing them in when stock price rises.

The second group consists of employees, presumably valued ones, who do their jobs well, but who might work even harder or smarter by having the incentive of ownership in the enterprise. While giving options to employees may provide positive motivation, it may not always be the best way to compensate valued employees because the level of their compensation depends only on stock price increases, which they can't control, rather than on factors they can control.

> *Investors should understand that if a company issues significant stock options to employees, it signals that the investors' return will be limited.*

Why Are Options Issued?

Essentially, options are issued for four reasons. They can compensate for performance, offer incentives to improve performance, change behavior, or obscure actual compensation.

Using options to simply provide additional compensation makes little sense because there is no way to know how much compensation is being offered. Remember, the reported value of options when they are granted often bears no relationship to actual value realized. Recipients could easily be paid far more than estimated amounts (in a market bubble or if earnings are inflated), or they could be paid far less or not at all in a declining market.

As start-ups and struggling new comers, Amazon.com and many other high-tech firms used options as a way to compensate for their then lower-than-market salaries, and rank-and-file employees took them, banking on future stock price increases.

Making use of options as an incentive to change behavior makes sense as long as employees and managers work harder to

Making use of options as an incentive makes sense as long as employees and managers work harder to achieve objectives that are aligned with investors' interests.

achieve objectives that are aligned with investors' interests. Investors should question how much "incentive" is useful. Most executives work hard and do their best because they have an internal work ethic and self-standard of excellence. It is unlikely that the effort applied increases indefinitely with incentive pay. What is clear is that incentive pay changes behavior—the application of effort. The widespread use of options is questionable when one accepts that raising stock price is not always a constructive primary objective. Increasing the real value of the company will result in higher stock price over the long run (assuming growth outweighs dilution). But it makes little sense to provide incentive to change behavior to focus solely on increasing stock price instead of long-term value, and options have been structured to do just that.

In discussions with numerous compensation committees about large option grants, a troublesome consistency has emerged. Most members of these committees have said that they suspect that if their CEOs had been paid in cash at the same levels at which they were compensated through options, that shareholders would likely have rebelled. Whether or not they would have cannot be proven, but the fact that compensation committees have participated in keeping such information opaque from shareholders is troublesome indeed. One suspects that a primary purpose of options has been to provide "stealth" compensation to executives.

How Are Options Structured?

Minute-to-minute, stock price seldom reflects actual long-term value. But over extended periods, they tend to trend together. Constructing options so that profits cannot be realized for extended time periods will more likely result in returns that

SOURCE: "WHO GOT THE MOST FROM EXERCISING OPTIONS" *THE WALL STREET JOURNAL* (DECEMBER 17, 2002) SEC. B, PP. 1, 3.

FIGURE 3-1

Executives' Gains
From Exercising Options

EXECUTIVE NAME	BIGGEST RECENT GAIN FROM OPTIONS EXERCISE
Lawrence Ellison, Oracle	$706,076,907 (FY01)
Michael Eisner, Walt Disney	$569,827,702 (FY98)
Michael Dell, Dell Computer	$233,283,432 (FY99)
Sanford Weill, Citigroup	$220,162,892 (FY97)
Thomas Siebel, Siebel Systems	$174,613,276 (FY01)
Stephen Case, AOL Time Warner	$158,056,501 (FY97)
John Chambers, Cisco Systems	$155,980,290 (FY00)
Gerald Levin, AOL Time Warner	$152,590,000 (FY00)
Jozef Straus, JDS Uniphase	$150,295,997 (FY01)
Howard Solomon, Forest Laboratories	$147,252,540 (FY00)
Richard Fairbank, Capital One Financial	$142,231,274 (FY01)
Dennis Kozlowski, Tyco International	$139,739,099 (FY99)
Henry Silverman, Cendant	$129,146,928 (2000)
Kenneth Lay, Enron	$123,399,478 (2000)
David Pottruck, Charles Schwab & Co.	$118,900,210 (1999)
Louis Gerstner, Jr., IBM	$115,130,197 (2001)
Craig Barrett, Intel	$114,231,947 (1998)
Kevin Kalkhoven, JDS Uniphase	$106,171,030 (FY00)
Roberto Goizueta, Coca-Cola	$104,371,866 (1997)
Ralph Roberts, Comcast	$102,833,384 (1999)

approximate real growth in value.

Unfortunately, options have often been structured in ways that provide windfalls to a select few executives. **FIGURE 3-1** lists the individuals who were the largest exercisers of options between 1992 and 2002. According to the *Wall Street Journal*, the source of the figures, "On balance, many of the executives were able to time these exercises to the peak of the stock price, while shareholders who held on longer lost value." The newspaper also notes that the gain cited is "pretax and on paper—though it is typically counted as part of an executive's overall net worth and compensation."[1] Although the article did not say how companies report executive compensation, major gains in executive compensation can usually be found in a firm's SEC filings. Because they do not occur every year, however, such windfalls do not normally appear in reports that purport to show executive or director compensation.

One counter to the windfall profits problem would be to structure stock options programs for senior executives in such a way that they would not be able to sell those shares until a time when they have no ability to influence share price. If they can't profit from their shares until after they have left the company, they have much less incentive to influence share price in the short term.

CHAPTER 4 # The Share Price Game

POSSIBLY THE MOST COMMON LAMENT heard among share-holders following a dramatic downturn in the value of the shares they own in a company is, "Why didn't I sell when the stock was at its high, and everyone else was buying?" The recent past has shown us several possible answers:

A. Getting out at the top would have been sheer luck. The deck was stacked against you from the start.

B. The company failed to provide you with accurate and complete information about value and risk.

C. The research analysts you relied on were biased.

D. Executives intentionally managed the company's share price so they could profit from stock options.

E. Fundamental change lowered value, but you didn't realize it in time to sell.

F. All of the above.

In many cases, the answer would also include more about the role of directors and management. It could be written this way: "The company's directors and management were simply confused about their real responsibilities and perhaps unaware of or unconcerned about the inevitability of share price corrections. While they may have benefited at your expense, they did not premeditate that outcome. Nevertheless, you paid the price for their confusion and the poor corporate governance that resulted."

While pondering their plight, investors should also remember that they bear some personal responsibility for their lamentable situation. The inaccuracy and incompleteness of information during the tech bubble of the 1990s was obvious, but investors chose to ignore that fact while markets soared and paper wealth accumulated. Some experts, including Federal Reserve Chairman Alan Greenspan and billionaire investor Warren Buffett, warned about the dangers of excessive speculation in the markets, but investors generally turned a deaf ear, choosing instead to believe the executives who assured them that all was well.

> *There are two basic strategies for the Share Price Game: the offensive strategy of maximizing investor perceptions of future growth, and the defensive strategy of minimizing their perceptions of risk.*

When the euphoric markets plunged in 2000 and declined through early 2003, investors continued to shun logic and turned to hope and faith, waiting for the rebound. They took comfort in their presumed "knowledge" that a company's markets, revenues, and earnings always recover quickly. They could defend that position because analysts and media commentators sent messages that the market would recover.

Why did people think they could count on rising share prices and therefore not care about dividend yields? Why would they believe that companies were not subject to cycles of rapid growth followed by average or even mediocre growth? Why would they think that companies were immune to macroeconomic trends and geopolitical forces?

The answer is simple. They wanted to believe in the promise of sustained high growth with low risk, and that made them easy targets and willing pawns in the Share Price Game. The Game evolved first with the participation of a small number of executives and CEOs later joined by many others, all having a single-minded focus on steadily rising quarterly earnings. At annual meetings and conferences during the late 1980s, before the Game was business as usual, you could see these CEOs steering Wall Street and institutional investors toward a focus on the earnings numbers. By then, some already had the financial incentives in place to profit from this approach. Other CEOs who were not the instigators of the Game became willing players when they realized it could also turn them into heroes—rich heroes.

Playing the Game

STOCK PRICES DEPEND on perceptions of growth and risk. Decisions to buy or sell are to a large extent based on emotions, primarily greed and fear. Unlike hard facts, perceptions and emotions are easy to manipulate. Hard facts can be manipulated only by telling half-truths or lies. It is not surprising, therefore, that otherwise rational people let their emotions take over and were caught up in playing the Share Price Game.

The Game's goal is to manage or influence stock price to increasingly higher levels without necessarily creating commensurate real value in the enterprise. The price of a company's shares always moves back toward or through the real value level (see FIGURE 4-1). It can, however, deviate significantly and for extended periods, if management single-mindedly sets out to manage share price and investor emotions dominate logical analysis. The result: Share price is actually one of the easiest variables for management to control. This makes playing the Share Price Game even more seductive and rewarding, at least in the short term, for those who can control the numbers and "spin" the story. One caveat about the Share Price Game from the outset, however: It's always doomed to failure, since eventually executives will run out of plausible explanations. Investor emotions of euphoria and greed reverse to dismay and fear.

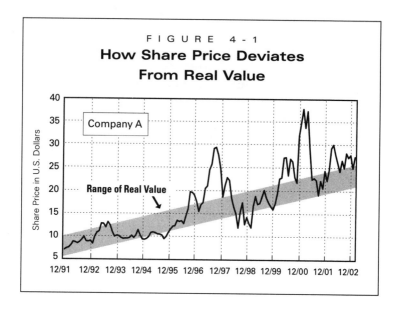

FIGURE 4-1

How Share Price Deviates From Real Value

The Playbooks

THERE ARE TWO BASIC STRATEGIES for the Share Price Game: the *offensive* strategy of maximizing investor perceptions of and confidence in sustained future growth, and the *defensive* strategy of minimizing their perceptions of risk. Both come complete with a playbook that companies use selectively depending on how the Game is progressing.

The Offensive Playbook

Here's how the offense develops:

- **Set aggressive growth targets and commit publicly to meet them.** Some CEOs indicate that their companies will grow indefinitely at a given, often unrealistically high, rate. Others simply provide guidance that implies it.

- **Meet quarterly earnings targets at all costs.** To set this play in motion, CEOs accelerate earnings or manufacture them to meet stated objectives.

- **Redefine the meaning of earnings.** If they can't stay on target, CEOs may apply a selective definition of earnings, for example, as operating earnings, pro forma earnings, core earnings, adjusted earnings, EBITDA, or any other type of "earnings before anything bad."
- **Default to another target metric.** If net income or other measures of earnings become too difficult to control, CEOs may try to brag about revenue, number of subscribers, miles of cable, or another number that they can control.
- **Adjust business practices.** Some CEOs will take this tack to stay on target, even if it means destroying real value.
- **Initiate stock buybacks to support share price, project management's options value, and manage earnings per share.** If stock price falls, management can raise it by buying out other shareholders at the depressed price.
- **Move stock price temporarily.** Management can time their personal transactions by adjusting quarterly earnings guidance and then exceeding or just meeting that guidance to indicate short-term acceleration or deceleration of growth. They can also control the disclosure of positive or negative news.

The Defensive Playbook

The purpose of defensive plays in the Share Price Game is to minimize investors' perception of risk:

- **Mitigate earnings volatility and earnings surprises.** The purpose of this play is to make earnings growth appear as smooth as possible. It requires management to spin a story about why earnings growth is steady and then to carefully manage and manufacture earnings to meet the expectations they've set. Although these stories may have a grain of truth to them, the whole truth often is much less rosy than investors are led to believe. You can never eliminate cyclical factors, insulate the company from competition, or suspend company development life cycles indefinitely.
- **Hide liabilities that increase financial risk.** Management can use such tactics as off-balance-sheet special purpose subsidiaries,

derivative structures, leasing transactions, and selective disclosure, to name just a few.

- **Obfuscate business risks.** When disclosure of certain business risks is mandatory but would prompt investors to question the sustainability of earnings and growth, management may include the information in boilerplate language, which is routinely dismissed as a response to overregulation.
- **Spin the best story possible.** Standard practice for this play includes enlisting the support of sell-side research analysts, specifically guided and indirectly paid for by the company through investment banking fees. This play also uses the business and popular media, especially television, to broadcast the company's stories far and wide.
- **Perpetuate the CEOs image of "infallibility."** A continuous barrage of favorable articles, news reports, and guest appearances featuring a "star" executive helps sustain investors' confidence and enhances the credibility of the manager's earnings guidance.

Companies may feel compelled to play the Share Price Game and investors may become caught up in its momentum, but sooner or later, the Game will end with severe penalties for the majority of the players. Investors get fried, they lose trust in the executives, and send them packing. The value of the stock (and stock options) dive as well. The road to this inevitable end begins with managing earnings expectations, but quickly deteriorates into manufacturing earnings, and in the worst cases, committing fraud. Chapter 5 details the landmarks along this winding and treacherous path.

Managing Earnings Expectations

WHETHER OR NOT quarterly earnings meet consensus expectations is central to the Share Price Game. Because quarterly earnings has become the most important measure in determining stock price, meeting quarterly earnings targets implies that a company is meeting its publicly stated overall growth targets and will continue to do so. Conversely, missing quarterly earnings targets, even by a few cents per share, has dire implications for a company.

Sometimes earnings growth cannot be maintained in the short run until additional reserves can be established or the macroeconomic environment improves. When this happens, executives can resort to managing investors' expectations of long-term growth. They do this by lowering forecasted quarterly earnings estimates through "whisper numbers" communicated to analysts. Then they exceed these lowered estimates and declare that the company did better than expected. Thus they not only maintain long-term expectations of sustained growth but also reinforce the infallibility of management to deliver on its promises.

Investors understand, at some level at least, that executives are playing the Share Price Game and that the company will do virtually anything to avoid missing the consensus forecast. A miss would imply that management had no other possible way to maintain the appearance of growth on schedule. The amazing thing about the Share Price Game is that investors know they are participants in it but remain addicted.

The Greater Fool Theory

When investors are told to expect high historical growth rates to continue indefinitely and to consider the risk of lower growth to be minimal, the Greater Fool Theory of investing replaces a more reasoned approach. One investor counts on another investor to pay a higher price for the stock based on future expectation of higher profits, sustained growth, and low perceived risk. An investor makes money off a stock in two ways: from dividends and from appreciation of the stock price. The price of a stock ultimately depends on the stream of future dividends that the stock will pay. But as the dividend yield (dividend amount relative to stock price) decreases, the appreciated value at which investors expect to sell the stock at a future date contributes a larger portion of the expected investment return and therefore drives current stock price. In the case where stocks pay no dividends, this estimated appreciation comprises the total return. When share-holders are not taking money off the table in the form of dividends, they remain wholly dependent on the relationship between the buy and sell price for their return.

One can look at these two profit components and how they are affected by the Greater Fool Theory in two different scenarios.

Investing Scenario #1

The assumption behind this first scenario is that both the buy price and the sell price of stocks accurately reflect real sustainable value based on full disclosure and full understanding by all investors. Stock price appreciates, therefore, as a result of real growth, real productivity enhancement, and real risk return assessment. This means that as fundamental value increases or decreases, stock price generally follows suit. A lack of dividends is acceptable to investors under this model because the likelihood of catastrophic events is low. It breaks down when stock price does not reflect real value.

Scenario #1 depends, of course, on something called *efficient market theory*. Throughout the 1970s and 1980s, prestigious U.S. colleges and universities taught that improved communication ensured that all relevant "facts" were known to a sufficient number of market participants, that the market adjusted almost simultaneously, and that stock prices reflected "truth" with regard to real value.

Professional traders and investors never fully bought into this idealistic view. They knew that they could beat the market not only by doing better analysis, but also by gaining access to better information or by correctly assessing the temporary influence of investor emotions. These same groups, however, generally agreed that in the absence of systematic nondisclosure or misleading information, the capital allocation system functioned reasonably well.

Investing Scenario #2

The second scenario says that neither the buy price nor the sell price must accurately reflect real value. As long as the perception of growth is maintained and risk is minimized, the share price will rise. This model is predicated on a lack of full disclosure and depends on earnings management and a healthy dose of spin control. Investors rely on rising stock price instead of dividends to create investment returns.

From the investors' viewpoint this model breaks down when an unpredictable event occurs and the sell price suddenly moves to reflect the stock's long-term, sustainable value. This price may be substantially lower than an investor's buy price once the market loses confidence in management. Shocks like this take place when previously reported earnings have not been accurate, which means that assumed growth rates have also been skewed. They can also happen when previously undisclosed risks come to light, causing investors to increase their assumed discount rate.

How Stock Price Is Affected

The pattern of stock price movement varies significantly between these two models of capital allocation. In the first model, as a company grows rapidly and risk is controlled, its stock price will trend higher as strategy and execution convert opportunity to earning power, and more important, as confidence in the trend continues. The rise in stock price will not be a straight line. Investors will assess information and recognize new risks and opportunities that may affect the company's ability to pay future dividends. If management fails to reinvest and sustain growth from existing or new activities, the stock price may stop rising or even trend lower for long periods and possibly decline to zero. Some level of short-term volatility will certainly occur, but as all investors react to developments, dramatic swings in stock price will only result from real changes in opportunity or risk.

In the second model, as long as the perception of steady growth and minimal risk can be maintained to attract a Greater Fool, stock price generally will rise. Certainly there will be bumps, but to the extent that new risks are obfuscated and the perception of earnings growth is maintained, even when real growth does not occur, the rise may occur relatively steadily. The longer perception differs from reality and new Greater Fools enter the market, the more the stock price deviates from reality and the greater the correction will be when investors learn the truth.

A Practical Example

FIGURE 4-2 graphically illustrates the effects of the two models. In the case of Company A, stock price has not been managed. Although Company A is hypothetical, the stock price charts of many companies appear similar to the one shown. Using the price chart of a real company would have made a more powerful statement, but determining with certainty that stock price has not been managed is significantly more difficult than determining that it has. (In addition, few, if any, companies today would want to hold themselves up as a public example of purity.)

The second company shown in the exhibit is real: Tyco International. While Tyco has avoided bankruptcy, it personified earnings management and obfuscation abetted by a board that failed to notice what was going on until Tyco's businesses were unmasked as a group of average growth companies with little in common. CEO Dennis Kozlowski has been charged with fourteen

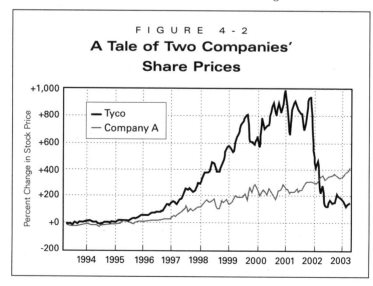

FIGURE 4-2
A Tale of Two Companies' Share Prices

CHART: www.BigCharts.com; © BigCharts.com

counts of sales tax evasion as well as corruption, conspiracy, grand larceny, and falsification of records.

One could logically conclude from the two charts that those who owned shares in Company A are undoubtedly a lot happier today than those who invested in Tyco. While prices were rising, investors understandably might have favored Tyco. But the end is always the same when earnings are managed and perceptions of risk are minimized. John Bogle, the founder and former CEO of The Vanguard Group, summed up this inevitability succinctly: "The fact is that when the perception (interim stock prices) vastly departs from the reality (intrinsic corporate values), the gap can *only* be reconciled in favor of reality."[1]

Why Stock Prices Rise and Fall

AS DISCUSSED EARLIER, most investors have as their ultimate investment objective to buy low and sell high. For this to happen, each investor who wants to sell a share of stock has to have a corresponding buyer who wants to buy that share at the higher price. What causes the price to rise and fall in value is the imbalance between demand and supply—buyers and sellers—in the market. Profitable investing, therefore, comes down to who gets it right about when to buy and when to sell. Over time, realizing investment returns that exceed the long-term increase in corporate profits, which historically has tracked with but has been less than GDP growth, is a zero-sum game. If one investor makes more than 5 or 6 percent annually, another makes less.

This is a fundamental concept of a capitalist system. Yet in the presence of weak corporate governance, stock price takes on a much less "fundamental" aura because many have been inflated so easily. Many investors may find this conclusion difficult to believe. Believe it. Many more may find it troubling. It is.

A few of the basic concepts of stock valuation tell the story. The rate of expected future earnings growth is the main determinant of stock price. Expectations of sustained growth are absolutely critical to rising stock price. Historical growth rates of one to five years are used as a proxy for the future growth rate, unless there is fundamental analysis forecasting a change. A rising growth rate over the short term often is projected out for the long term, causing large changes in stock price.

All other things equal, the more certain earnings growth seems, the more a stock price will rise. In the short term, a stock's price increases when the growth rate is perceived to accelerate, and the price declines when growth decelerates. This is both an absolute and a relative concept. Prices rise when growth increases absolutely *and* when growth is relatively better than anticipated, given changed circumstances. Dividends also play a role in stock price. As a company pays out a declining proportion of earnings as dividends, stock price increasingly becomes a function of expected appreciation instead of actual cash to be received.

Bubbles in the market as a whole (and for individual companies' stocks) happen when the Greater Fool Theory overcomes fundamental intrinsic value from dividends. Then stock price is established by what another Greater Fool will pay based on expectations of a rising stock price. In this game, the perception of growth must be maintained so that stock price does not revert to fundamental value.

How Prices Are Set

Stock price is a function of the expected dividends to be received during stock ownership plus the value that the stock can be sold for (terminal price), both adjusted for the time value of money and for the perceived risks (quantified by discount rates) of actually receiving a dividend and achieving the sell price.[2]

The appropriate discount rate is also a function of risk and the return available from alternative investments. It varies with the following:

- **The general level of interest rates that in part defines acceptable earnings rates.** For example, in the 1970s when interest rates were very high, expected earnings rates that would induce an investor to buy a stock were high because buying a bond produced high returns.

- **Uncertainty about the return that will actually be recognized.** Uncertainty creates risk: the higher the uncertainty, the higher the risk becomes, and the higher the appropriate discount rate will be.

The terminal price—the price at which an investor expects to sell the stock—is set in the market by future shareholders (sellers) and future prospective shareholders (buyers). They in turn will set their prices based on future expected dividends and a still more distant terminal value. That more distant terminal value will, of course, depend on an even more distant expectation of future dividends and terminal value. Following this logic, it can be demonstrated mathematically that stock price is a function of expected future dividends and discount rate only. FIGURE 4-3 shows a theoretical calculation of stock price.

Shareholders who do not receive dividends on the stock they

FIGURE   4 - 3

Stock Price as a Function of Expected Future Dividends and Discount Rate

This simplified formula for determining stock price as a function of expected future dividends and discount rate assumes that dividends are paid annually and grow steadily at a certain rate.

Stock Price = Expected Dividend Next Year/Discount Rate – Growth Rate

Suppose the expected dividend is $2, the discount rate is 10 percent, and the expected growth rate in future dividends is 6 percent. Using the formula above the stock price would be $50.

Stock Price = $2/.10 − .06

$\qquad$ = $2/.04

$\qquad$ = $50

Considerable research exists to demonstrate that over the long term, dividend-paying stocks outperform nondividend-paying stocks by a healthy margin.

own may question the theoretical result that only dividends are important. In recent history, many companies, including those that were valued most highly, have paid little or no dividends. Even at lower stock prices than the peak, the dividend yield today of under 2 percent is well below its long-term average of about 5 percent.

If dividends and their growth rate determine stock price, how can a stock that does not pay dividends be valued or have a value? Companies that reinvest in the business instead of paying dividends *must* increase their earnings power so that a larger dividend can be paid at some time in the future. Those larger dividends are then discounted back to present value to result in the stock price. Shareholders' unrealistic hope of future dividend payments was a major contributing factor to the tech bubble in the late 1990s.

Real Life Examples

An article in the December 27, 2002, *Wall Street Journal* sketches out an example of reinvesting profits instead of paying dividends to investors.[3] According to that report, five companies—Microsoft, Cisco, Intel, Dell, and Oracle—had accumulated $87.5 billion in cash and were seeking to reinvest it. Each of these companies has a reputation for being well managed and their business models and technologies were all considered to be successful. All have been particularly good at extracting cash from the businesses. Instead of paying dividends, however, they have returned value to their shareholders primarily in the form of higher stock prices. (Subsequent to publication of that article, Microsoft and Intel announced in early 2003 their intention to pay dividends, albeit nominal ones, on the expectation that dividends would become tax free for investors, and therefore make buying the stock more appealing.)

When investors purchase shares in such companies, they are betting not so much on growth from the traditional businesses as they are on how the companies will invest their cash to generate future growth. A skeptic could make the case that investments based on such reasoning are close cousins of risky venture capital companies.

The good news is that these companies have ongoing cash flow, experienced management, and in-depth knowledge of their industries. For investors to make an informed judgment about investing in these companies and to calculate the appropriate discount rate to apply, though, they need as much information as possible about how the companies will reinvest their cash. And even if management wants to supply such information, that kind of analysis is very difficult and carries its own risk. Without the information, when investors have little more than unwavering faith in management and technology on which to base their investment decisions, the result could well be severe volatility in stock price.

Why Companies Don't Pay Dividends

Management has had a defensibly good reason not to pay dividends. The way federal tax policy has been structured, dividends are taxed twice, once at the corporate level, and again when individual investors receive them. They are taxed at higher income rates than capital gains rates. As a result, investors have continued to behave in accordance with the Greater Fool Theory, depending on management to reallocate resources successfully to maintain growth without taking any money off the table in the form of dividend payments.

How does this play out in the real world? Take Cisco Systems as an example. According to the *New York Times*, January 8, 2003, Cisco had cash reserves of $1.43 per share, yet paid no dividend. Instead, Cisco committed to an $8 billion stock repurchase program, on a schedule only known to management, to support the stock price.[4] By implication, management felt it knew better than shareholders how to reinvest the investor's cash.

Cisco is not alone in its decision to keep its cash. AOL Time Warner, eBay, Dell Computer, Sun Microsystems, and even Yellow Corporation, a trucking company, pay no dividends. William D. Zollars, chairman of Yellow Corporation, said, "We will continue to buy back stock if we think it is undervalued."[5] Mr. Zollars owned options on 500,000 shares of Yellow Corporation at the end of 2001.

Despite the December 2002 announcement of President George W. Bush's proposal to eliminate dividend taxes, many companies indicated that this tax change would have no impact on their decisions not to pay dividends (Microsoft and Intel being notable exceptions). The good news is that investors are beginning to understand the impact of receiving no dividends. The bad news is that if double taxation is not repealed, Congress will continue to facilitate Greater Fool investing and periodic catastrophic losses. They should also know that considerable research exists to demonstrate that over the long term, dividend-paying stocks outperform nondividend paying stocks by a healthy margin.[6]

The Reality of Corporate Growth Rates

SOPHISTICATED INVESTORS USE the dividend/discount model to determine fundamental value of stocks. Most investors, however, simply determine an appropriate price/earnings (P/E) ratio and apply it to earnings. The P/E is a composite metric of expected growth and the risk of actually realizing that growth in dividends and/or terminal value. For both individual companies and for the market as a whole, P/E ratios vary far more than is justified by reasonable changes in expectations for future growth rates. Why? Because investors make their decisions based on greed and fear.

Since the mid 1900s, the average P/E of the S&P 500 Index has ranged between a low of around 5 to a high of around 35. This reflects a wide-swinging pendulum of pessimism and optimism about earnings growth and earnings sustainability for the index as a whole. Between 1995 and 2000 the P/E of the S&P

increased about 90 percent, rising from 18 to 34, or at a compound growth rate of about 11 percent annually. In that time the market rose at a compound rate of around 20 percent (9 percent growth in combined earnings and dividends—including inflation—plus the 11 percent growth in P/E).[7] More than half the rise in stock prices resulted from rising investor optimism regarding future growth and risk.

Productivity and earnings growth did, in fact, increase, and the economy remained surprisingly healthy. But growth rates for the whole economy did not double as investors were led to believe. Many executives promised double-digit growth rates when average growth could not exceed about 6 percent. However, they provided guidance consistent with their promises, managed and manufactured earnings, and redefined the meaning of earnings when required. As management minimized the perceptions of risk, greed overwhelmed fear, and the second scenario described earlier prevailed.

The three-year decline in the broad averages between 2000 and 2003 is easy to explain. Investors reevaluated actual historical growth rates as a measure of expected future rates. They reevaluated risk when hidden liabilities were discovered. And they reevaluated the confidence they had in executives and the boards of directors that oversee them.

The Alignment of GDP and Corporate Growth

As a practical matter, it is virtually impossible for corporate profits to grow for any extended period at a rate that meaningfully exceeds Gross Domestic Product (GDP). Since 1929, GDP has grown at a compound rate of 6.6 percent, far below the promised double-digit rate that so many corporate executives have promised. In fact, according to John Bogle, corporate profits have actually grown at a rate of only 5.6 percent, rarely growing in any year at less than 4.5 percent and never greater than 7 percent.[8]

Certainly some companies' growth will exceed market averages. But all companies (or a large sampling of them) will not, and in fact cannot. Over the last several decades, research analysts, basing their forecasts on growth targets and guidance provided by the 500 companies in the S&P 500 Index have predicted their average growth would exceed 11.5 percent. Actual growth was about 6 percent.

So much for the claim that only those few corporate overseers that have been caught are guilty, and everyone else is a victim of the loss of confidence. Maybe many of those companies that have become virtually extinct—Enron, WorldCom, and the myriad dot-coms—went that way because they lacked viable business models and not just because they played the Share Price Game. Still, investors should ask themselves which companies continue to play the Game but just have businesses sufficiently good enough that they can avoid insolvency when their numbers and forecasts come into question.

In addition, the explosion in the number of companies issuing financial restatements indicates that more than a few were cooking the books. According to an October 2002 U.S. General Accounting Office report, the number of listed companies restating financial statements each year has increased by nearly 250 percent since 1997.[9] It appears that about half of the restatements were prompted by the company, the other half prompted externally.

This is discouraging in light of the SEC's admission that while it was overseeing the boom of IPOs in the late 1990s, it focused less of its efforts on the financial statements of existing large-cap companies. As the SEC now concentrates on bigger, better-known companies, one might expect more restatements to be triggered.

Corporate Life Cycles

Even with recessions that result in temporary setbacks, the entire economy should grow at a reasonably steady pace as incremental increases in labor and capital fuel growth. The economy works by reallocating capital and labor to enterprises that are succeeding and by depriving resources to companies that are stagnating.

But the actual performance and prospects of companies

change constantly. As consumer preferences, industrial needs, and technologies evolve, individual stocks and sometimes entire industries reach an all-time high, then decline, and perhaps become obsolete. There is considerable evidence showing that companies experience a normal life cycle. After launching, they can grow rapidly as they exploit new demand or new technology. As they earn above average returns, competition increases and profitability declines as other companies allocate incremental capital and attract labor to the same activity. Alternative approaches and technology become focused on the opportunity. As a result, demand and supply is balanced, growth rates decline, and risks rise from competition and technological changes, forcing returns on capital to decline—first to average and then to below-average rates. In general, all companies face this threat. They can mitigate it only by successfully and consistently reallocating their own capital and resources to new opportunities. Over long spans of time, records indicate that the chance of continuing rapid growth of a single company appears poor at best.

Of course, the implication of this process is that very few companies grow at super-growth rates for extended periods of time, and companies with high growth rates are almost certain to decline. Because stock prices reflect projected growth rates that are five, ten, or twenty years in advance, an assumption of steady growth at high levels presumes continuing future success in taking business risk, which is uncertain and must be reflected in the discount rate. This is especially significant to an investor if the company does not pay dividends providing a return based on risks successfully taken so that future risks are relatively less critical. It also makes the Greater Fool Theory and the Share Price Game appear even more preposterous.

Stock buyback programs, as described earlier, can be used as a substitute for dividends. Investors who choose not to take some capital off the table by selling into these programs commit even further to the Greater Fool Theory. Ideally, stock-buybacks would be done when the share price was high, allowing investors to sell and take profits at the capital gains rate, which is better than the

Management would execute buybacks when prices dipped, encouraging a rebound. But that meant profit-taking investors were selling at a lower price, which hurt their returns. double taxation that dividends are subjected to. But that's not the way it has worked recently. Management has announced buybacks when prices dipped, encouraging a rebound. But that meant profit-taking investors were selling at a lower price, which hurt their returns. That's another sign management has other things on its mind than the good of all shareholders.

The Share Price Game, however, hides declining growth and maintains investors' perceptions of continuing future growth while obfuscating risks. This results in sudden, unpredictable, and very steep declines in price when investors realize that:

- historically reported growth was not real growth
- previously reported earnings were inflated
- current real earnings are much lower than investors were told
- management has been focusing on short-term reported results instead of long-term value creation and the reallocation of resources to new opportunities

Extending the Playing Time

AS PRICES ROLLED OVER and began heading down in 2000, in an effort to extend the Game and provide buying support, professional investment advisers on TV, sell-side researchers, the popular press, and corporate executives themselves began stressing the benefits of a buy-and-hold strategy. "Nothing to fear," they said. "Prices always go up." As prices declined further and many investors' paper profits became unrealized losses during the next two years, expert advice progressed to buying on the dips. "Just a profit opportunity," they said. Many executives supported that view, lamenting on TV that their stocks had declined significantly and were drastically undervalued. Regulators and market makers weighed in as well. Even the Chairman of the

New York Stock Exchange, Richard Grasso, joined the spin effort when he commented on NBC's *Meet The Press*, "I think investors, unfortunately, have been disappointed by a number of failures on the part of some companies to be truthful and honest with their investors, and the public's confidence has been tested. The market however ... has historically always responded to the economy. Our economy is strong."

The next wave of advice to investors was to "leg into investments," buying stocks on a schedule over time since "bottoms" are hard to predict. Did anyone ever advise investors about the wisdom of "legging out" while they had unrealized gains, noting that tops are also hard to predict?

Naturally, investors readily accepted all this expert advice because it promised exactly what they wanted to hear. Like everyone else, they relish being right. This common human trait can become a decided disadvantage, however, when making investment decisions. When an investor buys a stock and the price goes up, all is well. When the price falls part of the way back toward the purchase price, some investors continue to believe they are still right and do nothing. Others recognize that they were wrong not to sell at the top, but to reaffirm their rightness, wait for the stock to recover and once it recovers, they are right again and do not sell.

Sometimes when the price falls to a break-even level, investors sell. (Of course, selling shares at the same price at which they were bought never results in breakeven after taking into consideration transaction costs, inflation, and the time value of money.) More frequently, the pain of lost paper profits creates paralysis, and investors just hope their "rightness" will be reaffirmed. All advice that promises redemption is welcomed, and all advice to take a loss is rejected until the pain becomes unbearable.

Playing With Emotion

Despite deep analytical resources—better computing power and independent third-party research on the Internet—most individual investors make their buy or sell decisions based almost exclusively on emotion. Professional investors and traders are more disciplined, but they also often cling to an old idea in the place of new logic. Greed fueled the Share Price Game for a long time, and fear caused a rapid collapse when many sold their shares after prices had declined below the investment price.

In exchange for participating in the luxury of liquid capital markets, all investors pay the price of having the value of their savings (and therefore the level of their future lifestyle) recalculated minute by minute. When a relatively small percentage of everyone's savings was in equity securities, most investors in the market did not track their investments daily. Once more investors had a greater stake in volatile equity stocks, and television constantly tracked their ups and downs, investing became far more emotional. The Share Price Game capitalized on the resulting euphoria on the way up. Investors have paid the price on the way down. Emotional investing is stressful, but that's an inherent part of the Game.

Assessing the Landscape

The broad-based increases in P/E ratios described earlier demonstrate a significant rise in expectations about future performance. This should cause investors to question the contention of many "experts" that the excesses of Tyco, WorldCom, Enron, and others are isolated cases and not the common practices of most companies.

Many executives lament that the market has given them a "no confidence" vote, asserting that they are completely innocent of reporting inflated earnings, raising investor expectations beyond realistic levels, and thereby encouraging an emotional and speculative bubble. Certainly, some executives can legitimately make these assertions. Still others may be culpable in the Share Price Game, but have stopped well short of committing fraud, have consistently reported results in conformity to GAAP, and have acted in what they perceived to be the best interests of shareholders. But this does not necessarily make them innocent of contributing to the bubble and the losses that investors have experienced. After the biggest run-up of stock prices in history, many investors were lucky simply to break even. As paper profits soared in the 1990s, investors spent on better lifestyles financed with debt. That debt now has to be repaid, and future investing will be fueled by an increased sense of desperation.

Critical questions remain to be answered. Will investors consider whether they would have been better off if prices had not diverged so dramatically from real value? Or will they still buy into the Greater Fool Theory and remain willing pawns in the Stock Price Game? With the stakes higher than ever, will executives, directors, politicians, the media, and investment advisers of all kinds try to prevent another bubble and restore some sanity? Or will they try the same old tricks? Now is our chance to make change and follow better practices for the health of the markets and suffering investors.

CHAPTER 5 # How to Spot When the Game Is in Play

Understanding who participates—executives, directors, analysts, and investors—in the Share Price Game is one thing. Digging into the details of how those executives so skillfully manage, manufacture, make up, and redefine earnings is quite another. Knowing the mechanics and how to recognize them is as critical for directors (the fiduciaries of all shareholders) as it is for shareholders and prospective investors who want to make informed decisions about how they allocate their capital.

You'll see in this chapter that management has wide latitude in reporting quarterly revenues and earnings within the confines of Generally Accepted Accounting Principles (GAAP). Executives have even wider latitude when they choose not to conform to GAAP, which more than a few have done under pressure to report consistent growth quarter after quarter.

In the real world, when such hanky-panky becomes public knowledge, share prices decline steeply and rapidly in their return to more realistic levels. The revelations do not usually result from rigorous analysis by investors. It's usually some external event that suddenly awakens investors, and they begin to lose their unwavering optimism. These stock price time lines shown in FIGURES 1-1 through 1-5 in Chapter 1 show examples of such events and how they track quite closely with stock price movement. These situations force investors to take a closer look at earnings quality, historical growth, and risk. Only then does the truth become clear, and for most investors, that clarity comes too late.

The Problem With Quarterly Earnings

AS DISCUSSED IN CHAPTER 4, capital in liquid markets is allocated based on investors' expectations of what future stock prices will be. Those expectations are based on information investors glean from any number of sources, but the most important are company-produced financial data and annual reports. Most people appear to take these at face value, which gives the company tremendous information leverage.[1] When the reported numbers do not truly reflect the actual financial performance of the company—and when investors rely on those numbers alone to make critical investment decisions—sooner or later someone's going to get hurt.

With all the pressure they're under to meet or beat market expectations about earnings—and in doing so protect themselves and their livelihood—executives often spend a lot of time and energy on managing quarterly earnings. The business decisions they make, therefore, can have more to do with the earnings they will report next quarter than with building real value in the company long term.

Managing earnings is a tricky business. It may start out as a well-intentioned effort to reduce stock price volatility and, in a certain sense, to protect shareholders' interest. Unchecked, those good intentions can become the proverbial paving stones to a far more sinister place. This road from earnings management to earnings manufacture and sometimes to fraud is not necessarily a straight one, but taking that first step can be treacherous. Warning signs along the road read something like this:

- **"Smoothing" earnings.** Execs don't actually exaggerate total earnings growth, but by lowering the likelihood of earnings surprises, they can mitigate quarterly stock price volatility and bolster investor confidence in the company's future prospects. If their earnings are never off by more than a few pennies from the consensus figure, or if they are promising continual high growth in the face of a deteriorating environment, take note.

- **Manufacturing earnings.** If executives run out of ways or opportunities to manage earnings, they may resort to manufacturing earnings by systematically manipulating accounting and disclosure. In this case they exaggerate the reported growth rate, usually with the intent of increasing stock price. Questions to ask: Is earnings growth really outpacing revenue growth? And does the CEO keep talking about what seems like an untenable, long-term growth rate?

- **"Financial irregularities."** Even though serious misstatements in overall earnings may result from earnings manufacture, proving that the misstatement was intentional can be difficult, especially if earnings were manufactured in conformity with someone's interpretation of GAAP rules. If management has in fact misrepresented earnings with intent, the misstatement is called a financial irregularity—often a polite word for fraud.

Gaming GAAP

GENERALLY ACCEPTED ACCOUNTING PRINCIPLES (GAAP) is a very complex set of rules that determine how revenues and expenses are matched and how assets and liabilities are valued at a point in time. Because these rules and their interpretation are complex and subject to judgment, financial accounting can be used just as effectively to mismatch revenues and expenses as it can be to match them correctly—especially if one is willing to hide facts.

It is beyond the scope of this book to provide a detailed dissertation on GAAP accounting. However, investors should have a very basic understanding of the difference between what accounting is *believed* to do (represent truth) and what it can be *used* to do (obfuscate truth).

A Few Basics of Accrual Accounting

People often judge whether they are getting ahead or falling behind financially by whether they have more or less cash. Most individuals and many simple, privately owned businesses pay taxes on a cash basis—in other words, they count revenue when they get cash and they count expenses as they spend cash. But this method has a flaw: Cash may be received for work done in the past or not yet performed, and expenditures can be made in anticipation of work or subsequent to it.

For example, all businesses acquire some productive resources (called assets) to produce a product or service that is delivered later (resulting in revenue). Earnings are the result of matching revenues received in a specific period with the cost of the resources consumed in the same period (expenses). Assume that a person needs an automobile to perform services that bring in revenue. If that person buys a car today for cash, the expense would contribute to generating revenue for a long time. In such an instance, simply looking at cash flow would not be a good way to measure the person's profit and also fails to represent reality from a balance sheet perspective. An individual who uses cash (say, $30,000) to purchase a car would find in ten years that the car was certainly not worth the $30,000 originally paid.

Accrual accounting was developed to address these issues of matching revenue and expense and estimating the true value of assets and liabilities at any time. In the automobile example, the individual would have to see what the car was actually worth each year or, more reasonably, to estimate how much value the car was expected to lose each year. There would be no impact on the income statement when the car was purchased, but the expense would be recorded in subsequent periods as the value of the car declined.

Flexibility Within GAAP

GAAP provides significant latitude regarding when revenue and expenses are recognized and how they are matched. Implicit in virtually every line item shown on an income statement and balance sheet is a set of assumptions, estimates, or interpretations of rules. This means that every line item number lies somewhere within a continuum of possible numbers that conform to GAAP. There is never a "right" number. There are only numbers that are closer or further from an accurate description of the actual risks and performance of the enterprise. Similarly, the value of assets and liabilities can vary significantly within the bounds of GAAP.

GAAP can be used just as effectively to mismatch revenues and expenses as it can be to match them correctly— especially if one is willing to hide facts.

There is a legitimate need for flexibility to allow different companies to fully and fairly provide a set of financial statements that in total present a fair "picture" of their performance and financial condition. With the flexibility, however, comes the responsibility to use GAAP to tell the truth instead of to lie. All that investors can hope for is that all the assumptions, estimates, and GAAP interpretations combine to give them a fairly true picture of the company. A company's financial accounting can conform to GAAP and still result in a set of financial statements that are quite misleading. To make matters worse, large, powerful companies and entire industries actively lobby to expand the GAAP rules to give them more flexibility or to include loopholes.

In their book, *Building Public Trust: The Future of Corporate Reporting,* Sam DiPiazza, chief executive of Pricewaterhouse-Coopers, and Robert G. Eccles, president of Advisory Capital Partners, make a compelling argument for moving to more principles-based, rather than rules-based, accounting standards. They note, "Rules that are specific and clear can lead to adhering to the letter of the standard rather than to its spirit. Knowing precisely what you must do often defines precisely what you do not have to do."[2]

DiPiazza and Eccles say that although all accounting standards are based on principles, as clarifications have been requested, more and more rules of greater and greater specificity have been developed. They maintain that for standards "to remain true to the principles on which they are based, they must all focus on capturing and reporting the economic substance of a transaction." The authors also lay out five cornerstones for such standards: (1) Address issues of broad scope. (2) Reflect appropriately the economic substance of transactions. (3) Result in similar transactions being treated similarly. (4) Contain few, if any, alternatives, exceptions, or compromises. (5) Result in reporting and disclosure that are transparent and useful for decision making.

In an interview published in the *Financial Times,* June 18, 2002, DiPiazza said that the U.S. accounting system is replete with "exception upon exception" to appease companies or industries. He noted that many generally accepted accounting principles are six to eight pages long, but that exceptions can run to as many as 150 pages.[3]

When it is found that the company's previously reported financial performance was not reported in conformance to GAAP, it must restate its financial statements. If previously reported financial performance conformed to GAAP, yet turned out to be untrue because of poor assumptions, poor estimates, inappropriate accounting, or unexpected shocks, the company takes a write-off.

How often does this happen? According to the U.S. General Accounting Office report cited earlier, in the five years between 1997 and 2002, more than 850 publicly traded companies— about 10 percent of the total—restated their financial statements. Without a doubt, many more took write-offs. These are significant numbers, and undoubtedly statistics on restatements and write-offs will continue to rise.

The Really Bad News First

Accounting and the creative use of GAAP interpretations and exceptions can be used to accomplish four objectives:
- **Deferring or avoiding taxes.** Under GAAP, taxes can be deferred to later periods and very occasionally can be avoided

indefinitely. Deferral of taxes to later periods is generally considered to be a good thing because the company has the benefit of the cash not paid in taxes to invest in the business or elsewhere to earn a return until taxes are due. Deferred taxes will become due in the future, though, so accrual accounting requires their disclosure.

- **Shifting earnings to other periods.** Earnings can be moved from one period to another period. Usually they are accelerated and recognized earlier than they might be. This penalizes later earnings. Earnings management is the practice of decelerating earnings recognition and subsequently recognizing earnings "at will" to smooth out reported earnings.

- **Minimizing the perception of risk.** Companies can manipulate GAAP to understate, hide, or blur liabilities. Investors then are in danger of making investment decisions they would not have made if risk had been fully reported.

- **Manufacturing earnings.** Earnings manufacture—possible under GAAP—is the undisclosed, systematic acceleration of earnings and/or obfuscation of liabilities in order to report earnings growth. To accomplish exaggerated but smooth earnings growth resulting in a higher and higher base of reported earnings each period, an increasing level of profit has to be manufactured or actually earned each period. The bubble of manufactured earnings always bursts, sooner or later.

Fraud Is Easy

Fraud is a relatively easy concept for most people to grasp. Even if they don't understand all its complexities and vagaries, they know what it looks like when someone points it out to them. Unfortunately, the allegations of fraud have become increasingly common: Adelphia, Tyco, Enron, WorldCom, Sensormatic, Bankers Trust, Interpublic Group of Companies, Global Crossing, Lucent, Xerox, McKesson, Rite Aid, Computer Associates, Lernout and Hauspie, Livent, HealthSouth, and far too many more. Newspaper headlines reported it dramatically: "WorldCom Finds Accounting Fraud."[4] "Enron Target of

Criminal Probe."[5] "SEC to File Fraud Suit Against Xerox."[6] Lucent Stock Tumbles Over Fraud Inquiry."[7] "Rite Aid Ex-Officials Charged in Accounting Fraud Probe."[8]

The legal system has rightfully made the burden of proof for fraud very high, and the courts will ultimately decide who committed it and who didn't. As unfair as it seems, whatever the verdict may be, reasonable people will no doubt suspect that something fraudulent has occurred. They also should understand that few managers start out to commit fraud: they often simply find themselves on a slippery slope and end up where fraud begins.

The Slippery Slope

ALEX BERENSON, writing in the *New York Times* in the summer of 2002 at the end of Jack Welch's CEO tenure, noted, "For years, Wall Street has known that companies manage their earnings. Some companies, like General Electric, almost always seem to beat estimates by a penny or two a share, no matter what the economic climate."[9] Real trouble begins, however, when earnings management starts to descend toward earnings manufacture. When that happens investors are virtually guaranteed to come face-to-face with very significant declines in share price at some point. The only question is when they will and which of those investors will still be shareholders in the company when it happens.

Creating an Earnings Reserve

Earnings management is having earnings that could have been reported but were not, in order to create an earnings reserve. Picture this as a bucket labeled "earnings" that management fills up over time and then can dip into when needed. Managers can do this when they need to report numbers higher than those reflected in the actual earning period. Because the bucket never really goes totally empty, overall earnings are never exaggerated and, when viewed over time, the company's growth rate is not exaggerated. This is the simplified model of earnings management that companies admit to practicing. Here, however, the growth rate would be understated if there were still earnings in the bucket, and investors would have been harmed because share price would not be at its full potential value.

Of course, the level of earnings in the bucket at any point in time is never disclosed. Neither do companies report whether or not they've poured some additional earnings into or dipped some out. To do so would defeat the purpose of earnings management. If one could monitor additions and subtractions to the reserves, actual earnings instead of reported earnings could be and would be calculated.

That is why the earnings reserves kept in the bucket differ in principle from the type of reserves normally recognized by GAAP. Companies usually disclose the reserves recognized by GAAP at the time they are established, along with the level of the reserves and how much has been used. They are less diligent at reporting what should have been used. Earnings management reserves, on the other hand, are not disclosed and in fact do not exist officially until managers need them.

In practice, earnings management can deteriorate into earnings manufacture quite rapidly. At first, managers may create earnings by changing their accounting policies or by adjusting their accounting estimates and assumptions. For example, they can adopt progressively more aggressive GAAP interpretations, but still be in conformity to GAAP. Obviously, companies should have the ability to adopt an accounting convention that conforms to GAAP if that change reflects reality, even if it is a more aggressive interpretation that increases a period's earnings or earnings in all periods going forward. They may have very legitimate reasons to do so. A change in accounting practices does not necessarily indicate earnings manufacture, but an undisclosed accounting change that comes to light at a later time will most likely point to earnings manufacture. A series of new accounting interpretations that all result in higher earnings should raise the possibility of earnings manufacture. The pressure builds as they continue to follow these practices period after period, until what they may have thought of as "benignly" managed earnings turns into something more serious.

Michael Young, author of *Accounting Irregularities and Financial Fraud: A Corporate Governance Guide* (Aspen Publishers, Inc., 2001), succinctly describes the danger of managed earnings and its likely deterioration to manufactured earnings when top management establishes a culture that embraces earnings management. "Managerial acceptance of managed earnings, and in particular cookie jar reserves, can send an extraordinarily dangerous message to the troops: 'Where it is for the good of the corporate enterprise, it is all right to camouflage the truth.' Once that genie is out of the bottle, it will never go back. Managers at all levels will perceive themselves as having the license, if not the encouragement, to do what they have internally tried to resist all along—camouflage their own dismal inadequacies by subtle rearrangement of the numbers."[10]

> *In GAAP, there is never a "right" number. There are only numbers that are closer or farther from an accurate description of the actual risks and performance of the enterprise.*

A thorough understanding of why decisions were made and their impact is needed to identify the patterns and trends and to distinguish between earnings management and earnings manufacture. A pattern of more aggressive accounting interpretations is sometimes referred to as deteriorating "quality of earnings." Not surprisingly, quality of earnings is often associated with the risk of whether earnings levels can be sustained; a company with poor earnings quality has less cushion. In other words, managers find it harder to fill the bucket because they've already manufactured earnings, and they become hard pressed to find new manufacturing methods. The insidious nature of manufactured earnings rests in the fact that management can justify within GAAP each individual interpretation that resulted in the appearance of extra earnings.

All this should make investors very suspicious of executives who proclaim that the business will grow steadily at some rate year after year. By setting an earnings growth goal, and announcing it publicly, they have defined their own success and failure, and one would expect they would do "whatever it takes" to meet their goal.

The Trouble With Managed Earnings

Assume, for argument's sake, that a company has the discipline to only manage earnings. They fill the bucket with earnings that they have not recognized but could have, and dip into the bucket to smooth earnings as needed, never allowing the bucket to go dry. Management justifies changing accounting estimates and assumptions because changes presumably both help and hurt earnings over time. The argued benefit is that investors will experience less stock price variability as earnings consistently increase at a certain rate. As investors perceive the stock to be less risky, it will trade at a premium price.

The problem with this argument is that investors buy and sell their stock constantly. By managing earnings, companies deny investors accurate information about the real earnings of a company at all times. Companies might counter that because all investors are equally denied information, the playing field remains level, and no investor is disadvantaged by this lack of transparency. Investors are buying and selling for reasons other than the difference between actual and reported earnings, so harm is randomly allocated. If in fact there is always some level of earnings available in the bucket, one could argue that all investors have been equally harmed because actual earnings were really higher than reported.

Although earnings management may disadvantage all investors equally, the reason they are disadvantaged is because performance of their investments becomes a function of random timing or someone having inside information rather than because they have great insight or do superior analysis. Everyone is disadvantaged because incremental capital is allocated based on the promise of false earnings and growth at the expense of better real opportunities. In truth, not all shareholders are disadvantaged by earnings management: Insiders who own stock or options (and who know the real results and the real growth rates) have a clear advantage over outside investors.

Case Study I: Coca-Cola

THE COCA-COLA COMPANY'S example shows that through the efforts of an enlightened CEO and a strong board of directors the Share Price Game can be stopped.

Executives of Coca-Cola, playing a relatively simple form of the Game, in conformance with GAAP, helped to increase the price of the stock from around $20 per share in 1994 to a high of more than $86 in mid-1998. (See FIGURE 5-1.) Coke manufactures and markets the syrup for the company's beverages under the Coca-Cola brand name. This activity is not capital intensive. Coke's bottling operations combine the syrup with carbonated water and deliver the product—both very capital intensive, low-margin aspects of the business. To enhance earnings, the company began in 1986 to bundle up its bottling operations and spin them off. Coca-Cola Enterprises was the first and the largest of these operations. Coke retained 49 percent ownership,[11] but claimed that the company did not control the bottling operations, which meant that under GAAP they would not be part of consolidated financial results. But in practice, the bottlers were effectively single-supplier captives of Coke, and Coke directors dominated the boards. In fact, Doug Ivester, before becoming CEO of Coca-Cola, was chairman of Coca-Cola Enterprises, and approximately half of that company's board had close ties to Coke.

Coke loaded up the bottlers with its debt, and charged higher prices for its syrup, which raised Coke's margins while depressing the bottlers' margins. The company also "sold" distribution rights, generating income for Coke and goodwill for the bottlers. Coke guided its investors to look at its earnings growth and lack of risk. When asked about its "investment" in Coca-Cola

Enterprises, Coke urged investors to look at "cash operating profit," a fancy name for earnings before interest, taxes, depreciation and amortization (EBITDA), because interest, depreciation, and amortization were very significant in these capital intensive, highly leveraged, goodwill-burdened businesses. The result was that growth in Coca-Cola Enterprises was similar to sales growth.

Generally, when a company plays the Share Price Game, some hard-to-predict, external event leads to the Game being revealed. In Coke's case, it was an unforeseen contamination scare and recall, international antitrust investigations, and a discrimination lawsuit. Only in the face of this bad news did investors and analysts look at the obvious. After all, the Game had been working well up to then. When the truth was revealed, Coke's stock price fell more than 50 percent. Doug Ivester, who by then had become CEO, received a $120 million exit package in December 1999.[12]

Douglas Daft took over as CEO in early 2000. Investors trusted he would end the Game until early on he promised them contin-

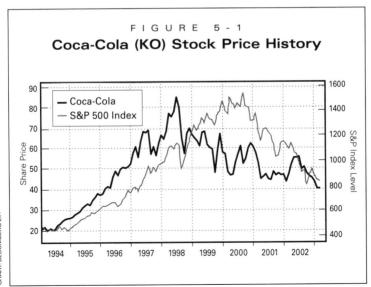

FIGURE 5-1

Coca-Cola (KO) Stock Price History

uous 15 percent earnings growth. With that, the stock slid back into the low $40s bottom, and hovered between $40 and $60 per share for the next three years. Smart investors will not fall for the same story too many times.

The lesson took hold. More recently Daft has been on the leading edge of good governance with encouragement from his board and in particular from Warren Buffett. Coke was one of the first companies to announce that options would be expensed going forward, and it later announced that it would no longer give quarterly earnings guidance.

The Coca-Cola case is reminiscent of what happened at Enron. Both Coca-Cola and Enron boosted profits by using nonconsolidated entities that they controlled as a practical matter. Not only did they put lower-margin or losing activities in these entities, they also further inflated profits by charging them for goods and services. These off-balance-sheet entities accepted the charges because of the control the companies exerted. In addition both Coca-Cola and Enron reported lower financial leverage risk by loading these nonconsolidated entities with debt.

There are, however, major differences between the two. Coca-Cola has a fundamentally sound business model, and management has run the business well, avoiding large mistakes. Enron's business model was flawed, and Enron management made a lot of bad investments. Enron held debt and booked interest expense in nonconsolidated special purpose entities while recognizing income at the Enron level. But Enron went much farther than Coca-Cola by obfuscating the existence and purpose of their off-balance-sheet subsidiaries. Coke did not try to hide the existence of its subsidiaries, but relied instead on trying to redefine growth in them and took the position that Coke did not control them.

In some instances where earnings manufacture has surfaced in very good companies, investors by and large have ignored it. Perhaps these were one-off events that did not indicate a pattern of behavior, or perhaps the company and its management succeeded in quickly allaying investor concerns. The lesson investors should take away from such an example, however, is clear. If they want to minimize their risk and sell their stock before possible price declines, they should watch diligently for warning signs of earnings manufacture and act accordingly.

Some Favorite Techniques

SOME REPRESENTATIVE EXAMPLES can help illustrate some of the more common methods for managing and manufacturing earnings and manipulating stock price.

Revenue Overstatement

Certainly the most straightforward method of overstating earnings is to overstate revenue. It's also one of the most typical financial statement fraud techniques, according to a research report issued by the Committee of Sponsoring Organizations of the Treadway Commission. The research, which set out to analyze financial fraud occurrences, found that in the companies studied, more than half of the frauds involved overstating revenues by recording them prematurely or fictitiously.[13] This practice comes in several forms.

Timing of revenue recognition. The simplest way to goose earnings is to allot revenues to a given quarter even though they were not made during that period. Sensormatic Electronics, a security system manufacturer, provides a startlingly simple example. According to an August 1998 report in *USA Today,* on the last day of each quarter, the time clocks that stamped Sensormatic's product shipment dates would stop at 11:45 A.M. The company continued making and shipping product, however, until they had reached their quarterly earnings targets. Then the clocks would start up again. In March 1998, Sensormatic settled fraud and false-reporting charges with the SEC, without admitting or denying any wrongdoing.[14]

More recently, Computer Associates, a software maker based in Long Island, New York, came under investigation as a result of claims by former employees that the company routinely backdated and forward-dated customer contracts to move earnings from one quarter to the next in an effort to meet earnings targets. One former employee said, "It was a longstanding practice at CA to keep the books open for weeks after the end of the quarter" to allow finance officials latitude to shift revenue between periods. The investigation was still ongoing as this book went to press.

Channel stuffing. Used primarily by manufacturers of tangible goods, channel stuffing essentially means flooding distributors and resellers with more product than they can or plan to sell. This boosts revenue in the current quarter by stealing it from future quarters.

One of the most benign, and perfectly legal, methods of channel stuffing is to offer customers greater incentives to order at a specific time, for example by discounting prices on larger orders or by simply discounting at the end of the month. Some channel stuffers, however, conspire with customers and distributors to take shipments of product that will never be sold in the future. After these sales have been booked, the customer returns the unsold product to the manufacturer for a full refund. A variation on the theme: Don't bill the customer for the goods, and then write off the receivable as a bad debt expense at some point in the future.[15]

Sunbeam Corp., the Florida-based company once headed by "Chainsaw" Al Dunlap (who got his nickname by cutting the companies he headed to the bone), was accused of channel stuffing in 1996 and 1997. Mr. Dunlap purportedly offered substantial discounts to retailers who placed orders for goods that they would not take delivery of for several months. Many times the product never left Sunbeam's warehouses. Mr. Dunlap was fired from the company and ordered to pay $15 million (without admitting or denying guilt) to settle investor lawsuits and SEC charges.

The *Wall Street Journal* reported that former executives at Bristol-Myers Squibb Co. outlined how the company used channel stuffing and other accounting tricks to boost current quarter earnings to meet financial targets. The company allegedly offered wholesalers incentives to buy more drugs than dictated by prescription demand. In the spring of 2002, Bristol-Myers admitted to the practice and, finding a scapegoat, promptly dismissed the executive in charge of the medicines group. During the year in which revenues were inflated, the former CEO sold stock from exercised options for over $70 million. Subsequently the company paid a $670 million fine to settle litigation related to illegally blocking generic competition. Both the head of research and the CFO quit.

According to an October 2002 U.S. General Accounting Office report, the number of listed companies restating financial statements has increased every year since 1997.

Sportswear retailer Cutter & Buck revealed in August 2002 that it had padded sales figures in 2000 by recording $5.8 million in shipments that were mostly returned, according to the *Seattle Times*. The article goes on to point out that one of the cofounders of the business, Joey Rodolfo, accused the company of shipping orders months before customers were expecting to take delivery. Mr. Rodolfo made this allegation just prior to leaving the company in 1997. Some customers and former employees say early shipments continued for years after Rodolfo left. For example, one sales representative indicated that clients in Florida, Georgia, and the Carolinas received shipments of fleece garments in May, although they had ordered them for delivery the next fall.[16]

Channel stuffing is very easy to detect. Proving that it is part of a fraudulent scheme is much more difficult. If growth in accounts receivables significantly outpaces the rate of sales growth, a good chance exists that some sort of forward sales have taken place. Of course, offering discounts on products at the end of a quarter or fiscal year is not an illegal practice. Asking clients to take delivery of products that they have every intention of never selling and are expecting to return is.

Churning revenues. Dynegy, CMS Energy, Reliant Resources, El Paso, Duke Energy, and others have all been accused of bogus round-trip energy trades designed to boost revenues. These trades are noteworthy for several reasons. First, many of the trades involved three or more participants. In more traditional revenue cases, only two parties would be involved. They were making trades at no profit and no loss to book trading volume (revenue) at each company, making it seem that there was a lot of activity. In many of the trading cases in question, three, four, or more companies conspired to inflate the revenues of all. Second, in many of the trades, the inflated revenue did not impact earnings, but had a very material impact on cash flow, and this is an industry judged on its top-line growth. Dynegy restated its 2001 financials, reducing cash flow from operations by $300 million.[17]

Cookie Jar Reserves

Companies may legitimately set aside monies in reserve accounts to allow for bad debts or other costs, such as restructuring charges that often occur in the operation of a business. When the company puts more money into the reserve account than it knows it will need, the money becomes "cookie jar reserves." When the reserve is created, it is classified as a one-time, non-recurring event. The company can then dip into the overage and add it back to operating earnings in future quarters. Xerox Corporation was accused of using cookie jar reserves to appear more profitable than it really was. The company was disciplined by the SEC for manipulating earnings (using this among many other techniques) and settled with the SEC without admitting wrongdoing.[18] (See the discussion of Xerox on page 99 and FIGURE 5.3.)

On November 4, 2002, *The Asian Wall Street Journal,* reported that the SEC was investigating whether Lucent intentionally overstated the size of a $2.6 billion pretax restructuring charge recorded in 1995, before its spin-off from AT&T, setting up a reserve account that could be dipped into later to bolster its bottom line.[19]

Microsoft used similar measures to understate its earnings by as much as $900 million over a four-year period, according to a June 4, 2002, report in the *Washington Post*. The SEC alleged that the use of the reserve accounts caused Microsoft to overstate its profits in some quarters and understate it in others. Microsoft settled by agreeing to stop the practice but did not admit or deny guilt. The SEC stated that it did not charge the company with fraud in part because the financial statements for the periods in question were more than three years old. The regulators couldn't prove that improper bookkeeping misled investors "to their detriment."[20] One might interpret this to mean that they could not identify harm with respect to specific investors.

Companies can also use reserve accounts to hide ill-gotten gains. Enron, for example, used undisclosed reserves to keep as much as $1.5 billion in trading profits off its income statement during the energy crisis in California. The reserves would have doubled the company's profits at a time when the California State and Federal governments were accusing energy companies, such as Enron, of price gouging. Enron then went on to use the huge reserves to smooth earnings reported to Wall Street and the credit rating agencies. Kenneth Lay and Jeff Skilling both claimed to know about the reserve accounts but stated the accounts were proper and used to guard against the likelihood of various California utility companies declaring bankruptcy.[21]

Assumptions and Estimates

Another way companies can manufacture earnings is by manipulating the assumptions and estimates that are integral to earnings calculations. Often they will disclose the changes, but rarely will they explain in reasonable detail the impact that the change will have.

A company ought to consider changing estimates and assumptions based on management's best judgment of reality. Sometimes they should be changed; at other times a change is not justifiable. These are judgment calls. Baruch Lev, an accounting professor at New York University who has testified before

Congress on accounting reform, uses Cisco Systems' bad debt reserves as an example of changing estimates and assumptions. In May 2002 the company reduced earnings by $346 million in anticipation of defaults, but it is impossible to tell if those defaults ever occurred. Actual defaults are buried in the next quarter's reserve. Somewhat with tongue in cheek, Lev notes, "That's the beauty of accounting. You don't see; they don't tell."[22]

Earnings assumptions and pension funds. Earnings assumptions are critical to pension fund accounting, but typically companies make very little data available to investors. A pension fund is considered to be underfunded or overfunded based on assumptions of future earnings on the stocks and bonds in the pension fund portfolio and the expected future benefits to be paid. If the fund is underfunded according to these assumptions, companies must record a liability to reflect that fact. The company can report some of the extra amount as income.

Throughout the 1990s, many companies assumed that earnings rates on pension funds would remain high or even rise. Granted, stock prices were rising, however interest rates were falling precipitously. (A significant portion of pension assets is in debt instruments.) When interest rates were at historical highs in the 1970s many pension funds purchased 30-year debt instruments with double-digit yields. Everyone knew that such yields could not be replaced in a low-interest environment using debt. However, based on the soaring equity markets, many companies not only continued to assume high earnings rates, but actually raised them and were able to report inflated earnings growth. Credit Suisse First Boston estimates that in 2000, 14 percent of reported earnings growth of the Fortune 500 came from pension income.[23]

Acquisition Accounting

Rather than creating a reserve earnings bucket by accounting for operations, some companies manufacture earnings through a one-time accounting treatment for one-time events such as acquisitions. They find it relatively easy to inflate earnings and growth rates, especially in rising markets, by issuing overpriced securities while overpaying for the businesses they acquire. Revenues and earnings per share show favorable growth rates until it becomes clear that the acquirer overpaid. Management then, of course, takes a one-time write-off and repeats the cycle by doing more deals. They continue to claim high growth "from operations," which of course is not from operations at all.

This play obviously ends as these overpayments for past deals catch up with the company. The acquirer's share price declines to real value levels. Reported growth then decelerates rapidly because new deals cannot be completed. The alternatives then are to sell assets or to take write-offs of goodwill. As companies become very large it is increasingly difficult to maintain growth through acquisitions because they must engineer bigger and bigger deals to maintain reported growth.

Example: one large deal. One high-profile example of overpaying for a large enterprise with inflated stock is JDS Uniphase Corp., which purchased SDL, Inc. in July 2000 for $41 billion in stock, increasing JDS's assets from $25 billion to $65 billion. The next year JDS took a one-time $50 billion write-off, decreasing its GAAP earnings by that amount, but carefully reported pro forma earnings that did not include the write-off. The company argued that the pro forma number better reflected ongoing earning power. That's possible, but JDS Uniphase investors were diluted by $41 billion in a company that produced less than $6 billion of revenues in the previous five years. In this case, one transaction made reported earnings meaningless. An even higher-profile example would be AOL Time Warner, which in 2002 wrote off a total of $98 billion following the $106 billion merger of the two companies.

Example: many small deals. Tyco achieved similar earnings growth using many small transactions. In late December 2002, the internal investigation concluded that its acquisition binge over the previous years had not resulted in a conglomeration of synergistic high-growth businesses, as the company claimed. Based largely on acquisitions, Tyco had reported earnings growth of approximately 20 percent for most of the previous decade.

Many acquisitions were not even disclosed. In the three years prior to Tyco's dramatic share price decline in the summer of 2002, the company completed more than 700 deals with an aggregate value in excess of $8 billion.[24]

A change in accounting practices does not necessarily indicate earnings manufacture, but an undisclosed accounting change that comes to light later usually does.

This was not disclosed because each deal alone was deemed "not material." An average transaction size of $11.5 million may or may not be material, but surely $8 billion is. In addition, after Tyco acquired Raychem, a large West Coast company, e-mails indicated that Tyco had asked Raychem just prior to the acquisition to accelerate payments to its suppliers to reduce cash flow so that under Tyco's ownership cash flow would appear to accelerate. Tyco's response to all these revelations was typical and unsatisfying: "Accounting practices were consistent with generally accepted accounting practices."

The premiums Tyco paid for acquisitions are telling. Tyco spent an average 3.2 times revenue for companies it purchased but didn't disclose compared to 1.6 times revenue for the larger, disclosed transactions. While smaller deals often carry slightly higher multiples of revenue, the large spread clearly implies that management was more concerned with buying revenue and not having to disclose it than with spending shareholder money wisely.

A study for the *Wall Street Journal* by Thomson Financial revealed that stocks of the top fifty acquirers in the late 1990s fell approximately three times as much as the Dow Jones Industrial Average.[25] Should investors conclude that all acquisitions bode trouble? Of course not, but executives and directors certainly must bear the burden of explaining and justifying why they spend shareholder money to expand the business, especially into new businesses that weren't part of an investor's original "buy" calculation.

Other acquirers. There's a long list of other very aggressive acquirers. Cisco, for example, completed more than seventy acquisition deals in the 1990s. Its stock in 2003 was down about 80 percent from its high. General Electric spent more than $18 billion in 2001 and would have spent much more if it had been allowed to complete the acquisition of Honeywell (which was vetoed by the European Commission on Competition).

Vivendi Universal spent more than $100 billion on media companies and tried to unload many of them after its stock fell from $83.43 to $13.18 between June and late October 2002. Under French GAAP, the company incurred a noncash, one-time charge of 12.64 billion euros (roughly the same amount in U.S. dollars) of amortization of goodwill in certain acquired assets, including 6 billion for Canal+ and 1.3 billion for Universal Studios Group.[26]

WorldCom's share price declined 95 percent after the company made more than seventy acquisitions. The company's accounting practices (among many other activities) are under investigation. WorldCom has responded to criticism saying, "The company did not rely *solely* on acquisitions for growth" (emphasis added).

Big Baths and Restructuring Charges

Companies take "big baths" for one of three reasons. They find themselves in a bad financial situation that they can no longer hide from investors. Or, after an outgoing CEO has pushed earnings manufacture to the limit, the new CEO needs a reserve to assure his own success (and perhaps wealth). More seriously, financial results may already be so dismal that it makes sense to take all possible write-offs to build up cookie jar reserves for the future.

In all three cases, the stock first is beaten down by the write-off, which allows options to be issued at lower prices, and then future growth is promised to make the options appreciate. The logic here is that analysts and investors are going to beat up the stock anyhow, so why not include more expenses in the charge and work off of a smaller base next year? In most cases companies do not include the write-offs in the calculation of ongoing earnings reported to investors. They label them as one-time charges and not part of core or ongoing performance.

One common example of a big bath maneuver is an inventory write-down. In late April 2001, Cisco Systems reported that it would take a huge $1 billion plus write-down, basically stating that component parts in inventory were worthless because the company couldn't sell or use them. The write-down was considered an extraordinary, one-time item. Analysts therefore did not include the loss in earnings estimates or the valuation models that determine the price at which the company's stock should trade. Over time, as the components are built into switches, routers, and hubs, and those goods are sold, the inventory gradually gains its value back, adding to earnings of the company.[27]

More telling, Scott Sullivan, former CFO of WorldCom, planned to "take care of" many expenses that had been capitalized inappropriately by using a write-down of some sort. If Cynthia Cooper, vice president of internal audit, and her audit group had not uncovered the fraud, the ploy might have worked.[28]

In the acquisitive 1990s, many companies simply paid too much for the businesses they bought. With the decline in the stock market in the early 2000s, they chose to admit tacitly that they overpaid and to write-down the difference between the purchase price and the actual or book value of the company. Investors have a limited understanding of the extent of write-offs and their impact. In 2001, for all stocks in the S&P 500, companies wrote off income equal to about 40 percent of all reported profits.[29] Goldman Sachs estimated that write-offs for the Fortune 500 would be 60 percent of income reported in 2002, up from the 10 to 20 percent that prevailed for much of the 1990s. The average for the decade of the 1990s was around 20 percent, which means that about one-fifth of all reported profits in that ten-year period were later written off.

Glimmers of hope have begun to appear that investors will no longer tolerate this practice and that companies have realized that their integrity has suffered. Procter & Gamble announced that it would end an ongoing restructuring program it had begun in 1999. By June 2003, the company was expected to have written off as one-time restructuring charges between $3.6 billion and

$3.7 billion that was previously reported as operating profit. Beginning with the next fiscal year, Procter & Gamble will charge future restructuring expenses to income, estimated at $150 million to $200 million per year.[30]

Hiding Interest Expense

Yet another way companies increase earnings—by hiding interest payments—is to either increase the company's financial leverage without disclosing it, or to report declining leverage when it is not actually declining. They do this most often through

Investors have a limited understanding of the extent of write-offs and their impact. In 2001, S&P 500 companies wrote off income equal to about 40 percent of all reported profits.

"special purpose subsidiaries." The case study of Coca-Cola earlier in this chapter describes the method in detail. Like Enron, Coca-Cola held debt and booked interest expense in nonconsolidated, but effectively controlled, companies recognizing income at the parent level. Similar to Enron, Coca-Cola not only obfuscated the level of financial risk and hid interest expense, but also inflated profits by booking income through transfer pricing or by mispricing assets.

Capitalization of Costs

Accounting 101 teaches that capital costs, such as equipment, property, and other major purchases, can be depreciated over long periods of time. Operating costs such as salaries, benefits, and rent are subtracted from income on a quarterly basis and have an immediate impact on profits. If a company chose to capitalize an expense that was actually an operating cost, it would improve its current earnings by decreasing expenses in the current period. Generally speaking this rule leaves very little room for interpretation.

WorldCom, however, in an effort to boost flagging profits, classified certain line costs—expenses used to purchase time on communications wires—as capitalized costs, when they should have been treated them as operating expenses. When this scheme came to light, the company restated its earnings by more than $9 billion and ultimately sought Chapter 11 bankruptcy protection.

Pro Forma Earnings

Pro forma earnings are a close cousin to manufactured earnings. In some instances, when pro forma earnings are carefully defined, reported consistently over time, and not as a replacement for reported GAAP earnings, they can be valuable to knowledgeable investors. On the other hand, pro forma earnings can also be used to divert investor's attention to a different definition of earnings numbers when the opportunities for earnings manufacturing start running out and the traditional definition of earnings will no longer result in favorable comparisons. While GAAP earnings can be gamed and vary widely, they are at least constrained by some rules. Pro forma earnings have no rules, and the increasing use of them over the past few years has been nothing short of dramatic as **FIGURE 5-2** shows.

According to SmartStock Investor.com, companies in the Nasdaq 100 reported a loss for the first three quarters of 2001 of $82.3 billion. For the same period, these companies also reported pro forma earnings profit of $19.1 billion, a difference of more than $100 billion.[31] Applying any incremental price earnings multiple to $100 billion results in the possibility of a substantial correction when investors focus on GAAP or even adjusted GAAP numbers instead of whatever numbers are most favorable to the company.

Stock Buyback Programs

In addition to managing earnings, companies boost earnings per share by controlling the number of shares outstanding through stock buybacks. When companies consistently issue options to management, resulting in additional shares outstanding, share buyback programs are necessary to mask dilution to providers of capital as a group.

A secondary purpose of stock buyback programs is to support the company's stock price and hopefully to bid it up, create momentum, and to bolster investor confidence with a continuing trend of stock price appreciation. In short, the stock buyback strategy is to spend existing shareholder money to encourage other shareholders to invest or existing shareholders to invest more.

This has not always been the case, and undoubtedly some companies are employing stock repurchases responsibly today. Buybacks were legitimized in the 1980s as a way to return cash to some shareholders in a tax-efficient way. Because dividends, the traditional method of returning cash to shareholders, are taxed at regular income rates, it was argued that investors who wanted cash could realize it at capital gains rates through a buyback program.

Proponents of buybacks argued that companies that were obligated to reinvest cash to earn the best risk-adjusted return

F I G U R E   5 - 2
Companies Issuing Pro Forma Earnings Reports

YEAR	YEAR OVER YEAR % INCREASE	REPORTS OF PRO FORMA EARNINGS
2001	38%	1,468*
2000	71%	1,066
1999	(10)%	625
1998	6%	693
1997	30%	657
1996	32%	504
1995	495%	381
1990	49%	64
1985	378%	43
1980	NA	9

*Annualized number as of 7/1/2001 based on actual figure of 734.

SOURCE : GENE D'AVOLIO, EFI GILDOR, AND ANDREA SHLEIFER. TECHNOLOGY. INFORMATION PRODUCTION, AND MARKET EFFICIENCY." DRAFT PAPER, SEPTEMBER 18, 2001. HTTP://POST.ECONOMICS.HARVARD.EDU/FACULTY/SHLEIFER/PAPERS/TECHNOLOGY_PAPER_FINAL.PDF.

(and to provide cash returns to shareholders tax-effectively) could accomplish both by conducting ongoing buyback programs over time. If the company's management and board of directors determined that in their judgment the purchase of the company's stock at prevailing price levels would offer the best risk-adjusted return, then a stock buyback was reasonable and in the best interests of shareholders. Remaining shareholders benefited from a proportionally larger call on the income and assets of the business, and selling shareholders received relatively favorable tax treatment. Many would argue that this original justification has been stretched past reasonable limits. Consider the following:

- In practice, executives announce stock buybacks to signal their confidence in future earnings growth, and stock price increases, making buybacks a powerful weapon in their spin-control arsenals. The number and dollar volume of buybacks has increased dramatically, mirroring the increase in options granted. In 1991 approximately $25 billion in buybacks was made, compared to $200 billion in 2001. In July 2002 alone, as the market sank, more than 100 companies initiated over $43 billion in announced buyback programs.[32]

- Both announcements and actual stock purchases accelerate dramatically in overall market downdrafts, and usually within a day or so. Are investors to believe that when the entire market declines precipitously, and thousands of stocks trade lower, that boards can determine that purchasing their stock reasonably represents the best available investment? Following the October 1987 decline, 777 public companies announced repurchase programs. In September 2001, 193 companies announced buybacks totaling $54 billion.[33]

- Buybacks also serve to offset and mask the impact of dilution from employee option exercises. If employee stock is repurchased, the result is similar to simply paying employees more cash. If investor shares are repurchased, the result is that investors have transferred ownership to employees and at depressed prices if that is when buybacks are initiated.

* The opportunity for executives to time option grants and stock sales to benefit from price changes influenced by buyback programs is obvious. Because companies do not disclose the precise timing of either option grants or stock buybacks, it is difficult for investors to monitor such activities. Numerous services attempt to quantify such activity. One such study indicates that senior executives of IBM sold $35 million of IBM shares for a $14 million profit, selling 2.5 times as many shares as they acquired from new options, between October 1996 and March 1997. During those two quarters IBM bought $3.9 billion of its own stock, contributing significantly to its rise. The response of some of these executives was that nothing was illegal, and it is not. Whether it was ethical was not discussed.[34]

In the past, at least there was the pretense of a legitimate value-based decision in instituting stock buyback programs. Many large companies have reinvented them as a way to manipulate earnings per share, to meet their whisper numbers, and, in a few instances, to influence short-term price movements for the benefit of insiders.

Case Study II: Xerox

FOR FIFTEEN YEARS, from 1975 to 1992, Xerox Corporation's stock traded between about $5 and $14 per share. Looking at a long-term chart, one would think that it was a $10 a share stock. In late 1986, Paul Allaire became a director and in 1990, CEO. Like most CEOs of large companies, Allaire was well respected. He was a member of the Business Roundtable and Business Council and was on the board of directors of other companies including J.P. Morgan, Lucent Technologies, Sara Lee, Smith Kline, and Priceline.com.

Xerox's stock continued to trade in the same range until around 1994, at which time the price began to rise along with the general rise in the stock market. In 1997, approximately five years before Allaire's scheduled retirement, Xerox stock began to

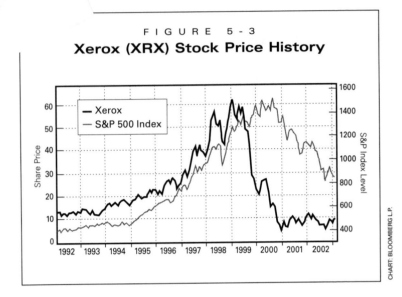

F I G U R E 5 - 3

Xerox (XRX) Stock Price History

CHART: BLOOMBERG L.P.

outperform the market. The stock reached a high of $63.69 on May 3, 1999 (see **FIGURE 5-3**). This was just one month after Allaire stepped aside as CEO and became Chairman, and Rick Thoman, with the support of Allaire, became CEO.

The 1999 Proxy Statement disclosed that Allaire had realized approximately $8.3 million on sales of stock from options in 1998. It also disclosed that he still owned approximately $57 million of exercisable options and $21 million of not yet exercisable options. For each 10 percent increase in the stock price, Allaire would make approximately $17.8 million, or for each $1 increase in share price he would make a little more than $3 million. Thoman's option position was less vested, but he had more upside over the longer run: For each 10 percent rise in stock price he would make approximately $27 million, or for each $1 increase in share price, he would make over $4 million. Both individuals clearly had a significant vested interest in the stock price.

Just one week prior to the shareholder meeting in May 1999, Xerox officials told Wall Street analysts that Xerox shares were undervalued given the company's "consistent earnings growth" of

"12 percent or better in 16 of the past 17 quarters," and that the company's goal would continue to be to "consistently deliver earnings growth of mid to high teens." In effect, the predicted growth bar was raised, and some wondered how profits could grow at three times the rate of revenues. Revenue growth was predicted to be 5 percent for the quarter although year-to-year revenue growth for the first quarter was zero.

Investors Grow Uneasy

By July investors were getting suspicious. In retrospect, they had good reason. The stock had fallen more than 10 percent when Xerox reported that it was in line with its targets for second-quarter growth of 13 percent in "core earnings." The company also noted that revenue had grown at only 2.5 percent and that "mid to high teens" earnings per share growth would be hard to achieve for the balance of the year. On receipt of that news, the stock traded down 8.2 percent to close just below $51. The company tried to adjust the spin to emphasize future opportunities, noting that it was transforming itself from a copier company to a copier services company and that it expected the services component to account for 50 percent of total revenue (up from 15 percent) within eight to ten years. Research analysts supported the company story. Eight out of eleven continued to rank Xerox a strong buy.

By mid-September 1999, Xerox was forced to lower expectations again when the CFO noted that revenue growth would fall below 5 percent. A strong U.S. dollar and economic weakness were blamed—although with the stock down about 30 percent from the high four months earlier, several analysts expressed doubt that Xerox's problems were limited to foreign sales. Within a week Xerox announced the acquisition of Tektronix's color printing and imaging business for $950 million, saying that it expected that market to grow at 23 percent for the next three years. Thoman said, "This is really about growth."[35] Again the analysts supported the company, noting that Xerox's problems were little more than a paper jam and that the Tektronix deal would catapult Xerox from number six to number two in the color printing and imaging business.

In October 1999, the company warned that third-quarter earnings would not meet expectations and that they would, in fact, decline more than 18 percent. The stock promptly traded down 25 percent to $30. The company again blamed weakness in foreign sales. Two months later, the company warned it would miss fourth-quarter earnings expectations by 40 percent, and Thoman declined to give guidance for 2000.[36] The stock traded down to under $25. Within a few more days it hit $20.

With the stock trading at about one-third the price of its high, some analysts lowered their ratings to a "hold," while one retained the "strong buy" rating and predicted the stock would hit $41 within eighteen months. The stock continued to decline throughout 2000 and closed at $4.69 on December 5, 2000, at which time there were ten "hold" recommendations and one "sell" recommendation on the stock. During the course of the year, as the price declined despite every effort by the company to hold it up, Allaire sold stock, which he had acquired from options, for more than $8.5 million.

In early 2000, the company announced a joint investigation with their auditors, KPMG, into accounting irregularities in Mexico. The investigation was headed by Thomas Theobald, chairman of the audit committee. In May Thoman retired as CEO, and Allaire was reappointed to replace him and given a two-year contract. At the same time the Board appointed Anne Mulcahy as President and COO. She had been with Xerox for twenty-five years, most recently as EVP of Xerox and President of General Market Operations.

By October 2000, Mulcahy had learned more about Xerox than she had bargained for. To her credit she proclaimed Xerox's business model to be "unsustainable," and the company's stock fell 25 percent in one day. She has said, in retrospect, that such a pronouncement taught her a "painful lesson" about disclosure.[37] Investors who might have but didn't buy stock that day avoided the pain of future price declines and probably applauded

Mulcahy's candor. Had they bought, their investment would have been reduced to half its value relatively quickly.

Six months later, more than one year after the beginning of the Mexico investigation, and after having delayed the filing of its 2000 10K in April 2001, the company finally filed on May 31, 2001. That filing disclosed the restatement of consolidated financial statements for two years ended December 31, 1998 and 1999. Net income for 1998 was reduced by $122 million (30.9 percent) and for 1999 by $85 million (6 percent). In total, that came to a $207 million overstatement of income.

The company acknowledged that certain accounting errors and irregularities had occurred, and that GAAP had been misapplied. The blame was placed squarely on several senior managers in Mexico who had collaborated to circumvent Xerox's accounting policies and procedures. Thoman, by virtue of his being replaced, was indirectly accused, and the board fired KPMG, which absorbed blame. Not mentioned was the fact that Xerox had complained previously to KPMG about an auditor who was questioning its accounting and requested that the individual be taken off the Xerox account.

The SEC Steps In

Unlike with other companies that have successfully swept problems away with minor disclosures, the SEC was not satisfied with these adjustments and continued its own investigation, which resulted in the commission filing a civil fraud injunctive action against Xerox in April 2002. The complaint alleged that Xerox had overstated revenues by more than $3 billion and profits by more than $1.5 billion over a four-year period beginning in 1997. This year coincided with the time that Xerox began to outperform the market and Allaire began to accumulate a fortune. The action was finally settled in June 2002 with a second restatement involving the inappropriate booking of $6.4 billion in revenue and overstated pretax profits of $1.4 billion.[38] The company was fined $10 million, paid, of course, with shareholders' money.

Stephen Cutler, the SEC's director of enforcement said,

"Xerox used its accounting to burnish and distort operating results rather than to describe them accurately. As a result, investors were misled and betrayed." Paul R. Berger, associate director of enforcement said, "Xerox's senior management orchestrated a four-year scheme to disguise the company's true operating performance.... Senior management had no compunctions about engaging in improper conduct." And Charles D. Neimeier, chief accountant for the division of enforcement added, "Xerox employed a wide variety of undisclosed and often improper top-side accounting actions to manage the quality of its reported earnings. As a result, the company created an illusion that its operating results were substantially better than they really were."[39]

FIGURE 5-4, based on a chart prepared by the SEC, shows the impact of the accounting manipulation at Xerox, quarter by quarter, for the years 1997 through 1999. The lowest part of each bar is real EPS. The smaller top component shows manufactured one-off earnings and the partial line near or at the top of each bar pinpoints the consensus analyst's estimates, largely guided by the company. This chart clearly demonstrates earnings manipulation. The SEC learned during its investigation that Xerox CFO Barry Romeril had told senior management in November 1999, "When accounting actions were stripped away, Xerox had essentially 'no growth' throughout the late 1990s."

The Aftermath

Rich Thoman retired after events caught up with him and he was unable to sustain reported growth. Thomas Theobald (who missed finding about $6 billion of overstated revenues and about $1.4 billion in overstated profits) resigned from the board in July 2002. Paul Allaire has not been prosecuted nor were his profits taken back, although the SEC has notified him that he may be subject to penalties. In 2001 he received a salary of $1.2 million and a bonus of $1.5 million, in total almost $1.5 million more than the previous year. Romeril, the CFO, retired at the end of 2001 and received a $500,000 termination bonus

Source: U.S. Securities and Exchange Commission news release, "Xerox Settles SEC Enforcement Action Charging Company With Fraud," April 11, 2002.

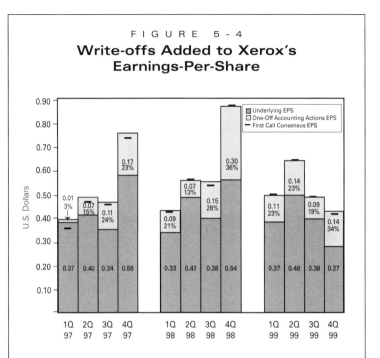

FIGURE 5-4

Write-offs Added to Xerox's Earnings-Per-Share

FIGURE 5-4 shows the impact of Xerox's one-off accounting actions on reported quarterly earnings per share 1997 through 1999. It also compares reported earnings per share with First Call consensus estimates by quarter.

as well as $1,215,000 for each of two years plus 50,000 incentive stock rights, from which he can profit if there is any recovery in share price. These terms, set by the board of directors, were more than his termination agreements required and were paid to "ensure a smooth transition." In his last working year he made less than $700,000.

Anne Mulcahy became CEO of Xerox in July 2001, the day after the company announced a $281 million second-quarter loss on a 13 percent decline in revenues. The stock was trading at $8. She became both Chairman and CEO on January 1, 2002, when Allaire retired.

The SEC settlement with Xerox occurred about six months after Enron went bankrupt. Although the Xerox case received several days of press coverage, the case was largely ignored by the media. When the settlement was announced, the stock was down 89 percent and was trading at $6.97, down from $63.69 at its high. In early 2003, *Corporate Financing Week* estimated that the company's pension fund was underfunded by $2.3 billion, which arguably should have been expensed over the period.[40] The primary difference between Enron and Xerox is that Xerox once had a viable business model and did not go bankrupt. To investors that lost money and employees who were fired, that difference is small.

Gaming GAAP Always Causes Harm

EARLY ON IN THIS BOOK, a caveat warned that the Share Price Game cannot go on forever. For investors, this warning should raise concerns about the consequences. Restoring financial health to a company that has played the Game and lost in the end is a difficult process, requiring substantial and prolonged pain for investors. Following the revelation that earnings have been manufactured, investors reassess reported earnings and earnings growth rates, both past and current. Then they extrapolate revised, lower historical growth rates into the future and the acceptable price/earnings ratio declines.

The combination of these two actions pushes stock prices down dramatically, leaving investors only with hope and a prayer for a rapid recovery. In most cases management and the board support this dream. They either dutifully take large write-offs, build cookie jar reserves, and fire thousands of employees to cut costs, or they look for other ways to manufacture more earnings. Thus, the cycle begins again.

But, when management chooses not to restart the Share Price Game and honestly tries to build real value in the company, recoveries are usually successful. They take a long time, and investors endure a long hangover, but the pain of price declines does not recur.

Why does performance languish for so long? To begin with, the questionable assumptions and estimates along with the timing differences that consistently accelerated earnings for several years must be reversed over time. This hampers real earnings growth because the accounting adjustments needed to reverse past damage come with a price tag. In addition, real financial and economic risk and damage must be reversed. If liabilities have been hidden, they must be paid off, diverting value from shareholders to lenders. Finally, changing any borderline business practices that were used to inflate earnings will come at some economic cost.

The message? Real value recoveries take time—years, not quarters. (The time frame of most executives does not extend to a great many years anymore, which makes the prospect of real recoveries less likely than investors would hope.) Everyone now has new choices to make. Reasonable investors can applaud more reasonable growth rates and accept that the short-term performance of a company will vary from quarter to quarter. Managements and boards can explicitly stop playing the Share Price Game with its earnings management and manufacture and focus instead on regaining real value. The alternative is not acceptable: another roller-coaster ride that will most likely end with even more pain.

CHAPTER 6 # The Balance of Power

DEMOCRATIC GOVERNMENTS ARE characterized by systems of checks and balances designed to prevent any one of government's branches—executive, legislative, or judiciary—from exerting excessive control. A major underlying assumption is that because the executive branch commands such power and has so many resources at its disposal, it must have close and continuous oversight. Corporations, like democracies, depend on checks and balances for essentially the same reasons.

In the U.S. government model, the Congress makes laws with which the executive branch must comply. The Congress also scrutinizes how the executive branch behaves to ensure that it does what it should. This happens through the work of congressional committees—for defense and intelligence, for example—and through the actions of Congress as a whole.

In the United Kingdom, which has a much longer history of checks and balances, the executive branch and even monarchs have faced many challenges arising from the checks and balances system. When Sir Thomas Moore tried to check King Henry VIII, he was executed. On the flip side, when King Charles I came to Parliament to arrest four lords who had challenged the king's total authority, Oliver Cromwell signed an execution order, and Charles lost his head.

Both the United States and the United Kingdom have put in place many mechanisms to enforce the accountability of leaders to the people they represent. In the United States, citizens choose their representatives through primary and general elections. They communicate directly with their congressional representatives. They can see and critique the voting records of individual representatives. They can even watch their elected representatives in action (or nonaction) by way of television broadcasts from the floors of both houses of Congress.

The idea that power must be checked and balanced has a long, colorful, even bloody history. And, rightfully, it continues to evolve to greater levels of disclosure and transparency. Government and governance both work best not only when those in positions of power scrutinize one other, but also when their constituents scrutinize the powerful as well.

Checks and Balances in Corporate Structure

JUST AS DEMOCRATIC GOVERNMENTS should serve the best interests of the electorate, a corporation should serve the best interests of its own constituencies, primarily its shareholders. Naturally, the interests of a company's other stakeholders—employees, communities, or other groups or individuals—must always be considered, and sometimes may even take primacy. In general, however, capitalism functions on the premise that putting the interests of investors first results in optimal capital allocation and productivity.

In the modern corporation, the parallels of "governance" to "government" are obvious. The executive branch of government corresponds to corporate executive management, and the congressional branch to the board of directors. The primary rights of shareholders and the obligations and responsibilities of both directors and management are well understood and clearly defined by law and by individual corporate guidelines. Though different organizations use slightly different language, the

Organization for Economic Cooperation and Development, the National Association of Corporate Director's Blue Ribbon Commission on Director Professionalism, the Business Roundtable, and others differentiate the roles and responsibilities of directors and executive management in much the same way.

What Boards of Directors Do

Boards of directors set corporate policy and establish and monitor "governance mechanisms" to assure that company systems and critical individual policies are consistent with overall corporate policy. They also have oversight responsibility for strategy and performance, including control of risks, both business and financial.

Setting policy includes establishing and maintaining the philosophy and mission of the company and ensuring ethical behavior and compliance with laws and regulations. Boards of directors have ultimate responsibility for the success or failure of the corporation because of their power and authority to

- hire and fire the CEO
- set executive compensation
- approve strategy and validate that the approved strategy is followed
- oversee risk and its control, both business and financial
- maintain a corporate culture of ethical behavior that limits risk and provides an environment conducive to success

Boards of directors fulfill these responsibilities through "governance mechanisms" that include all systems, policies, procedures, and processes used to collect and analyze performance information, and standards of behavior and values for the company and its employees. These governance mechanisms allow the board to perform its oversight duties and to monitor risk, the level and detail of the company's financial reporting and transparency, corporate social responsibility, environmental issues, and how key employees are compensated. These board responsibilities typically fall on the shoulders of six to twelve individuals working part-time for limited compensation in an environment dominated by the individuals they supposedly oversee— the managers.

What Management Does

Management, under the direction of the CEO, has direct responsibility for executing strategy and running the business day to day. This includes business and operational planning, strategy and business plan implementation, and all the daily decisions required to perform these tasks.

With regard to governance mechanisms, management is primarily responsible for internal controls, including the systematic identification and management of risks of all kinds. The output of this internal control function feeds into the governance mechanisms. These tasks and responsibilities fall to the CEO and executive management team, supported by extensive staffs, considerable resources, and outside advisers hired by management.

What Shareholders Do

Shareholders risk their hard-earned money by supplying capital to companies based on some level of understanding of the risks and opportunities of the enterprise. As shareholders have become numerous and dispersed, they have increasingly relied on boards to act as their fiduciaries. Shareholders, however, retain the power to sell their stock if they do not like the company's strategy or its execution. In addition, they theoretically elect directors and have the power to change the composition of the board if they feel the directors are not serving the interests of shareholders well. They can exercise this power in annual elections or through a proxy contest. To hold directors accountable, shareholders need a mechanism to assess the board's performance as a group and as individuals. That, in turn, requires that shareholders have accurate and timely information about what the board does and why.

For a company and its shareholders to prosper, all parties must work together. Because capitalism is based on self-interest, they must also look over each other's shoulders. They should not try to do each other's job, of course, but they should carefully scrutinize each other's performance.

Just as the executive branch of the federal government manages the ongoing affairs of a country, corporate executives must be empowered to manage a company day to day. They must also have the power to make critical decisions, sometimes very quickly, to ensure the company's viability and success. For example, corporate executives must certainly use their best judgment to make decisions that will protect the company from unforeseen economic adversity, respond to an aggressive or potentially harmful move by a competitor, or take advantage of opportunities as they arise. No company could long survive if every decision had to be submitted to the board, much less all of the company's shareholders, for a yea or nay vote.

Directors should question management thoroughly about strategy execution and report information on each individual director's record of performance.

This does not imply, however, that the power and responsibilities of the board (nor the will of the shareholders) can be subordinated routinely to executive management's whims or personal motives. While shareholders delegate enormous power to executive management, they expect that management will exercise its broad powers wisely and in the shareholders' best interest. They should trust management to do so, but management should recognize that such trust will be tenuous, at best, if shareholders cannot verify the quality and results of management's work.

If only because of their vast numbers and geographic dispersion, shareholders cannot supervise every move that management makes. Instead, they rely on the board of directors, which they elect—at least ostensibly—to do that for them. In theory and by law, the board is directly responsible and accountable to the electorate, and must ensure that the capital the investors have provided is safeguarded and used wisely.

In many cases that simply does not happen because the system of checks and balances supposedly inherent in corporate structure has failed. It has failed not because boards of directors have actually lost their power. In reality, checks and balances have failed because boards have never—or very rarely—actually held power, much less exercised it. Both corporate executives and directors have behaved as if the board's responsibility to monitor, scrutinize, and scrupulously question management's decisions and actions never existed, even though these responsibilities rank among the board's most important tasks.

Constructive Tension

The distinct duties and responsibilities of shareholders, directors, and management require different but specific authority, knowledge, information, and resources. Not only must all parties understand and accept their distinctive roles, they must all have profound respect for the value of sustaining healthy, productive governance relationships. Central to this is an understanding that some amount of tension and conflict are implicit in a checks and balances system.

For example, in fulfilling their strategy approval and verification roles, directors should question management thoroughly about strategy execution. In turn, so that shareholders can hold directors accountable, the board should report information on each individual director's record of performance. Real-life examples of such tensions are discussed throughout this book.

In the U.S. government, Congress and the executive branch benefit from tension and conflict. It differentiates the political parties and their individual members. Some might conclude that so much tension in government can at times impede progress. The opposite is the case in corporate governance. Recent revelations and events have clearly demonstrated that investors have been severely penalized by a complete lack of tension. Because directors are not really elected by shareholders, and their interests tend to align more closely with management, executives and directors avoid tension and by doing so destroy the checks and

balances system. Investors as well often fail in their checks and
balances role because of conflicts that can arise, for example,
when professional money managers serve individual investors
and also manage the pension plans of large corporations.

To a greater or lesser extent,
many CEOs and their management staffs have shifted the balance of power away from shareholders and directors and
toward management. Management has implicitly changed
policy, which boards of directors
are explicitly empowered to set.

*There is virtually no
effective mechanism for
communication between
shareholders of large
public companies and
boards of directors.*

They have changed corporate culture, redefined their mission as
one of managing share price instead of their companies' businesses, redefined acceptable ethical standards, and subjected their
companies to risks neither well understood by the board nor disclosed to its shareholders. In the process they have disenfran-
chised both shareholders and directors. When shareholders were
enjoying artificially inflated stock prices and when directors were
enjoying lucrative options and jetting around on corporate
expense accounts, neither group seemed to notice or care that the
balance of power had shifted to management. Today, they care.

Director/Shareholder Relationships

Do SHAREHOLDERS really have a meaningful relationship with
boards of directors? Basically, they don't. There is virtually no
effective mechanism for communication between shareholders of
large public companies and boards of directors. Most executives
actively discourage or even forbid independent directors from
communicating directly with shareholders. Likewise, shareholders have no real way to communicate with directors. A company's
annual report and SEC filings often fail to provide postal and
e-mail addresses, or phone numbers for directors. Annual meetings where shareholders are "invited" to see management and

directors are often held in out-of-the-way locations, making it more difficult for shareholders to attend.

Shareholders have very little influence over the composition of boards. Theoretically, a self-perpetuating nominating committee of the board puts together the slate of directors that shareholders will elect. In practice, however, there is only one candidate for each position, likely chosen by the CEO. Shareholders may vote for or against each candidate. And, by the way, candidates for the board know who votes for or against them.

Candidates for the board know who votes for or against them. This discourages institutional investors from voting their consciences because they get business from management and directors.

This alone can discourage institutional investors from voting their consciences because they need the support of management and directors to win business. Elections for directors have nothing akin to the constitutional right to privacy in popular elections.

Once the board is in place, shareholders have great difficulty in holding individual directors accountable for their actions. Virtually all votes taken by the board pass unanimously, usually because of pressure from other directors or the CEO. The directors that shareholders "elect" to bring wisdom, judgment, and experience to decision making on shareholders behalf virtually always agree with each other on all matters. Dissenting opinions are rarely put forward, certainly not in writing. Accountability is virtually nonexistent in this model.

Directors/CEO Relationships

THE RELATIONSHIPS between directors and CEOs certainly appear to be much closer than those between directors and shareholders. Directors, in fact, are often close friends with members of the management team and especially with CEOs. Such friendships are not inherently wrong as long as they are founded on respect for the distinct duties of each party and as long as they do not interfere with fiduciary responsibility. When friendships result in directors not adequately fulfilling their checks and balances role, however, problems can arise.

Although notable exceptions exist, most directors are nominated with the expectation that they will agree with the CEO unfailingly. In his book, *Take on the Street,* Arthur Levitt, former chairman of the SEC, describes how he was invited by Steve Jobs, Apple CEO, to join the company's board of directors. Prior to becoming a director, he made a visit to the company's San Jose, California, headquarters during which he gave the CFO a copy of a speech Levitt had given on corporate governance. When he departed he says, "I considered myself a part of the Apple family and looked forward to my first director's meeting with enthusiasm." The next day, however, Jobs told Levitt in a phone call that he had read the speech and, "Frankly, I think some of the issues you raised, while appropriate for some companies, really don't apply to Apple's culture." Levitt was uninvited to join the board.[1]

Unlike elected government officials, corporate directors are beholden for their jobs to the CEO and not to the shareholders/electorate, who in reality neither nominate nor elect the board. Not only do CEOs nominate directors, they also have a great deal of say about how directors are compensated. Then there's empathy. Many directors, having been CEOs themselves, understandably will sympathize with another CEO on management issues and challenges, despite their duty to represent the shareholders' interest. After all, directors who are CEOs themselves often have other CEOs on their own boards and would prefer not to set a precedent of interference with management.

Ultimately, although they don't actually have the power to fire a director, CEOs often have the ability to engineer the removal of a member of the board if that director fails to toe management's line Very few directors resist. In the few instances where individual directors have put up a fight, CEOs have generally prevailed, pointing out that such discord is not in the best interest of the company. These issues can be even more complex. If directors do not perform well, someone should remove them. But challenging or disagreeing with management does not in itself indicate poor performance. It can, in fact, indicate precisely the opposite. Situations may arise, however, when a director should be removed from the board for legitimate reasons. In such cases, CEOs may feel compelled to exercise their extraordinary power to do so because no other mechanism exists. Certainly shareholders can't do it. They lack any reliable way to assess board members' performance, and even if they did, they have virtually no power to remove directors when they perform poorly.

Should a CEO have the power to fire directors? When Jamie Dimon became CEO of troubled Bank One, he determined that in order to move ahead with the bank's turnaround, he would need a different kind of board. His solution? He exerted his authority by insisting on the resignation of most of the directors. In hindsight, in this instance he was justified in his actions. The bigger question remains: Are shareholders truly served well when CEOs can exercise such power over the shareholders' fiduciaries? Probably not.

The relationship between directors and CEOs, as it has evolved, seems convoluted. Directors serve to provide management oversight, but when the CEO holds the power to hire, pay, and fire directors, the director's ability to act independently is certainly compromised. Because independence is a hallmark of fiduciary responsibility, as discussed more fully in Chapter 7, anything that diminishes independence is a major governance problem.

Who Takes the Blame?

In deciding who should take the blame for specific instances of management or governance failures, the courts, regulatory agencies, the plaintiffs' bar, and the media will expend lots of effort, time, and money. Answering the broader question is easy: Everyone shares the blame.

Management has acted in its own self-interest, set policy, and changed governance. Directors have failed to protect investors but have not had the time, the resources, and apparently the will to fulfill their duty. Institutional investors have encouraged earnings management and seemingly ignored earnings manufacture. Conflicted research analysts and the investment banks that pay them have contributed to the ease of stock price manipulation. Auditors have relied on compliance with GAAP instead of a truly accurate accounting of performance and risk. Shareholders across the board have sat by while executives have taken free rein and directors have done little or nothing to prevent it. Until very recently, the SEC has been less than effective in putting its resources toward reviewing the financial statements of large cap companies to uncover financial irregularities.

There is no single, simple explanation for how and why executives have been able to shift the balance of power so decidedly in their favor. Rather, the answers lie in a complex set of interrelated factors, conditions, and behaviors that has given executives the opportunity, the incentives, and the ability to take control. These factors generally fall into three categories:

- Situations that enable executives to execute a dramatic power grab, thereby rendering directors virtually powerless
- Increased corporate complexity that allows executives to control, manipulate, and obfuscate financial and other performance information
- Shareholders' feelings of disenfranchisement that isolate them from their fiduciaries and prevent them from exerting their collective will

The CEO Power Grab

THE DURANTS' *The Lessons of History* makes a compelling argument that accumulating power and influence is a positive human trait.[2] If that is true, it makes sense that CEOs would strive to consolidate power, that shareholders would value their doing so, and that boards would put into power CEOs who can persevere in competitive situations. Such enormous, consolidated power, however, further underscores the need for an effective system of checks and balances.

The Power of Winning the Game

CEOs certainly have exerted their power in playing the Share Price Game. As discussed in Chapter 4, the Share Price Game is fairly easy to win for relatively short periods of time, and sometimes for five years or more. Shareholders (subscribers to the Greater Fool Theory, especially) want CEOs to win. Directors who served under CEOs who won during the market boom of the 1980s and 1990s became big financial winners as well. Once directors tacitly accepted earnings management and manufacture as legitimate management activities, they endorsed the strategies and tactics required to win the Game. By that time, it would have been inconceivable and inconsistent, if not impossible, for directors to try to curb the power of a CEO who had delivered such seemingly impressive results.

The Star Power of the CEO

CEOs who attain star status have little difficulty in exerting enormous power over their boards. When a CEO is singled out as the primary reason for a company's success, the board's ability to exert discipline is greatly curtailed.

From 1980 to 2000, the positive results that companies showed were directly attributed to the CEOs. This is somewhat ironic because common sense says that a company's success is the product of the cumulative efforts of many people—albeit under the leadership of the CEO. Nonetheless, CEO power and board weakness were propelled respectively to new heights and depths each time a headline lauded the achievements of star CEOs—such as Kozlowski, Welch, Messier, Ebbers, Bossidy, Gerstner, Lay, or Dolan. People should have been objectively reporting on the real performance of their companies—Tyco, GE, Vivendi, WorldCom, Allied Signal, Enron, or Bristol-Myers Squibb—instead.

With so many corporate leaders now stuck in the unflattering glare of the public spotlight, many reputable sources have proclaimed that the era of the star CEO is over. To paraphrase Mark Twain, the reports of the demise of the star CEO have been greatly exaggerated. As long ago as January 1993, an article in

Fortune magazine declared, "The King is Dead," and the "imperial CEO has had his day."[3] *Fortune* was just one among many respected publications that sounded the death knell over the next few years. In the November 3, 2002, issue of *Fortune* (again), Jerry Useem cited the publication's 1993 obituary and candidly surmised, "As we know now, the imperial CEO was not only alive and well but very much on the upslope of his career ... The more things change, the more creative CEOs get at turning circumstances to their advantage. In other words, they've got the power."[4]

> **Boards of directors should beware when a CEO achieves star status because their ability to discipline or replace that CEO is greatly compromised.**

So what's a board to do with a star CEO? It all depends. CEOs should shine, but for the right reason: not as managers of stock price, but as managers who build enduring value in their companies. Leadership and charisma are both star-making characteristics. Leadership is essential to continuously improving performance across the entire organization. Strong leaders provide the focus and direction a company needs to attain its goals, and they motivate others to perform well. Strong leaders set high standards of behavior and exemplify them by their own actions. Strong leadership also reduces uncertainty about the company's future and creates an environment where reasonable risks can be taken to deliver superior results.

Leadership combined with personal charisma instills confidence in the company's prospects. Such confidence is not only critical to a company's ongoing success, but also sets expectations of future results. Leadership and charisma in conjunction with full and honest disclosure is the most that shareholders could ask for in a chief executive.

Boards of directors should beware when a CEO achieves star status because their ability to discipline or replace that CEO is greatly compromised. If an excessive premium is built into the stock price primarily because of a star CEO, the cost to replace him can be high. Even if the board has legitimate reasons for wanting to make a change in CEO, they may feel hamstrung by the probability of a stock price decline in the near term. In such a case, the easy decision is no decision, and disclosing the dilemma to shareholders is not even a consideration.

Although Alan Ehrenhalt, editor of *Governing* magazine, was referring to politicians, his comment in the *New York Times* of September 30, 2002, rings equally true when applied to star CEOs: "The leaders we have trouble dealing with are those of obvious talent and genuine achievement who turn out to have displayed appalling ethical insensitivity—or worse."[5] John Randolph, a Virginia aristocrat and member of Congress in the 1820s, coined a phrase to describe people like Henry Clay who, he complained, was so brilliant, so capable and yet so corrupt that, "like a mackerel in the moonlight, he both shines and stinks."[6]

When it comes to their confidence in and the legitimacy of corporate leaders, investors are dealing with the mackerel in the moonlight issue. Unlike the case with politicians, bad behavior on the part of corporate executives can have immediate, direct, and quantifiable effects on their constituents—especially their investors and employees.

The Power of Compensation

The enormity of executive compensation clearly demonstrates the power that CEOs command. According to the Institute for Policy Studies' *Seventh Annual CEO Compensation Survey*, "Executive pay jumped 535% in the 1990s (before adjusting for inflation), far outstripping growth in the stock market (the S&P 500 rose 297%)." At the same time, the report goes on to say, workers' pay grew by only 32 percent, which barely outpaced inflation.

It's obvious that CEOs are getting a more than proportional share of companies' higher reported returns. Don't interpret this to mean that executives do not deserve excellent compensation. Those who build real value in the companies they lead should be paid handsomely for their performance. When compensation is not aligned with the right kind of performance, though, problems can arise. Those problems surely land most squarely at the feet of boards of directors who can control how executives are compensated. The Federal government has not made their job any easier. By limiting the deductibility of cash compensation to top executives, Congress during the Clinton administration encouraged the use of options as compensation, a primary driver of the Share Price Game.

Chapters 2 and 3 went into considerable detail about the issues that can surface when options become a major part of executive compensation. How major is major? The authors of *In the Company of Owners: The Truth about Stock Options,* Joseph Blasi, Douglas Kruse, and Aaron Bernstein, say that according to their calculations, "just the top five executives at the 1500 largest U.S. companies reaped a total of $18 billion in option profits in 2001."[7] For the entire decade of the 1990s, this group made a "collective total of about $58 billion." They add that as late as the end of 2000, after the stock market had declined so dramatically, "the top five officers in the largest U.S. companies would have pocketed a total of some $80 billion in profits if they could have exercised all those options at once." With so much at stake in terms of personal gain, one can easily understand why some greedy, unethical executives have taken as much as they could.

The Power of Information

To support and sustain their power over the corporation and the board of directors, many CEOs have circumvented governance mechanisms by supplying the board with information that is incomplete, inaccurate, or incomprehensible. They have prevented or discouraged directors from collecting independent outside information, meeting separately with internal and external auditors, and holding executive sessions of committees and the board. In a great show of reform, many companies are adopting guidelines to encourage such independent oversight from the board but have not empowered directors who continue to be deprived of time and resources.

A Power Base of Outside Experts

CEOs have found valuable allies for consolidating their power in the form of outside advisers and experts. While some experts have vigorously resisted the decline of good governance or have contributed meaningful solutions to the shareholders' dilemma, others have simply been part of the problem. Much has been written and said about the problems and potential conflicts of interest that can arise when a company's independent audit firm also provides outside consultation and advice to the company's management. In recognition of this potential for conflict, regulatory and legal impediments, including provisions within the Sarbanes-Oxley Act of 2002, prevent auditors from providing general consulting advice to their audit clients, and the major audit firms have complied.

Until the passage of Sarbanes-Oxley, many audit firms generally reported to management. The clear requirement in the legislation is that auditors report to the audit committee of the board. This means that auditors are far more likely to alert the board to potential irregularities than they previously were. This may, in fact, turn out to be a significant factor in improving governance because it recognizes that boards need to have auditors working and reporting to them instead of to management.

Less well reported is the role of compensation and succession-planning consultants. Frequently CEOs engage their own compensation consultants to "advise" the board on what the CEO should be paid (of course, the company, not the CEO, pays for this advice), and the typical result is a rapid escalation in pay. How does this come about? The most important consideration seems to be what CEOs of comparable companies make, and the definition of "comparable" can easily be gamed to point to a higher "comparable" salary.

CEOs have also found power-building and power-sustaining allies in many, but not all, corporate governance experts. Over the past decade or so, some attorneys and university professors have promoted themselves as governance experts, and some have come to fairly high levels of prominence in corporate governance circles.

As consultants, they are paid by companies and report to CEOs. Another category of expertise can be found in professional organizations that are directly controlled by or composed of CEOs. The Business Roundtable, for example, presents itself as an organization dedicated to good governance and routinely offers advice on the subject. Not surprisingly, this body of CEOs has consistently taken the side of executive management. In the past it has supported options as the primary component of compensation and opposed putting all stock option plans to shareholder votes or expensing options. It has opposed the separation of the CEO and board chairman positions, and only recently endorsed the concept that a majority of a board should be independent directors. Faced with continuing corporate scandals, the Business Roundtable has, to its credit, reversed many of those earlier positions.

Other governance experts, including members of various Blue Ribbon Commissions on corporate governance, have endorsed concepts of a single person serving as CEO and Chairman, the absolute and overriding necessity of friendly relationships between the board and CEO, and the predominant use of options to compensate both executives and directors.

As corporate governance has become an increasingly hot public relations topic, many companies have hired in-house governance experts and proclaimed with great fanfare their commitment to better governance. These staff experts report to the CEO. Undoubtedly many of them are very intelligent and well-meaning, but one can reasonably wonder whether a governance expert who reports to the CEO can operate effectively or independently in the interests of shareholders.

Corporate governance experts reporting to management can serve a very useful purpose: to collect and analyze information, benchmark performance, and provide a third-party perspective on the interrelated and complicated topics that directors face. Having such expertise available helps both directors and management to stay better informed, to share and agree on relevant information, to identify value drivers of the business, and to help identify and organize key issues.

To give shareholders the assurance that expert advice is being used in their best interests, it makes sense for experts to be hired by directors and report to them, whether for financial expertise, audit committee support, compensation advice, succession planning, or other corporate governance issues. Such experts can coordinate with those reporting to management to ensure that issues are vetted from all perspectives. This process can often resolve tensions and improve governance through information, analysis, and discussion.

The Complexity of the Modern Corporation

THE SHEER COMPLEXITY of modern corporations has created opportunities for executives to shift the balance of power away from boards. Today's major corporations are not simple widget makers. They are enormous, global enterprises with widely diverse products and services and complex corporate and financial structures. They are dynamic organizations, changing constantly, which makes them very difficult to understand.

Complexity enables executives to manage and manufacture earnings and to play the Share Price Game. When investors, directors, and analysts don't truly understand in detail how value is being created and accounted for, executives can hide the bad things and manufacture good things more easily. Spinning their stories is easier and verifying the truth is more difficult. A common lament among directors of late has been that "they didn't know." The more details there are to know and understand, the easier it becomes for executives to get shareholders and directors to buy into their story. Directors recognize that the businesses they oversee are complex. Many simply accept that they do not understand the business. Executives assert, "I know the facts and I know what we're doing, so don't question me."

The following discussion describes the most significant ways in which companies have become exponentially more complex. In some instances, however, management has exaggerated the complexity or purposefully created it to hide the truth about the company's performance.

Complex Corporate Structures

Corporate structures often become complex for very legitimate reasons: favorable tax treatment, limited liability, and the desire to include partners, to name a few. Some corporate structures, however, have become complex by design to make them difficult to understand and to enable chicanery. Complex structures give executives greater flexibility in manipulating and reporting financial results

> *Warren Buffet, in his 2003 letter to shareholders, called derivatives "financial weapons of mass destruction, carrying out dangers that while now latent are potentially lethal."*

and the ability to walk a fine line in terms of GAAP compliance. Some of the smartest people in the country, lawyers and investment bankers included, make very good wages advising companies on how to do those very things.

Consolidating financial statements through these complex structures and ultimately reporting on them publicly are formidable tasks. Internal and independent accountants and auditors know quite well that they can no longer check each and every bookkeeping entry. They rely instead on systems to spot-check that the financial roll-up complies with GAAP in theory. This gives considerable wiggle room for interpretation in the gray areas of accounting or for committing outright fraud.

The Enron scandal focused a great deal of attention on off-balance-sheet subsidiaries. While they are not unusual and may have legitimate purposes, they are also subject to abuse. Fully disclosing them would help, but to verify that they indeed serve a legitimate purpose, directors would need a deep level of understanding of the details. This challenge isn't limited to off-balance-sheet subsidiaries. On-balance-sheet subsidiaries come with a high degree of complexity as well, and large corporations have thousands of them.

Globalization

Virtually every country in the world has its own unique currency, financial institutions, regulations, and laws. Accounting principles and practices vary widely around the world, creating greater complexity in understanding the performance of global corporations. All that is further compounded by the lack of international standards for measuring and reporting corporate performance, even among competing companies in the same industry. On the darker side, tacit acceptance or tolerance of corruption in some countries greatly complicates doing business there, not to mention the difficulties it creates for accurately reporting risks and opportunities.

Proliferation of Financial Instruments

The last two decades witnessed an explosion of financial engineering and financial products. They include derivatives, finite financial products, insurance products, and a multitude of others with almost incomprehensible acronyms including MITTs, ABCs, LYONS, and MIPS. Not only do these products look like alphabet soup on paper, they are also extremely difficult to understand. Some experienced executives will even admit that the explanations of these products are simply impossible to decipher. While some have legitimate benefits—risk transfer for example—many others are designed to cloud information or enable the management and manipulation of reported financial results. Some, apparently, are just plain dangerous. Warren Buffet, in his annual letter to shareholders in 2003 called derivative contracts "financial weapons of mass destruction, carrying out dangers that while now latent are potentially lethal."[8]

Generally Accepted Accounting Principles

In the United States, GAAP becomes more complex every year, with many rules running to thirty or more pages, complete with multiple exceptions for accounting treatments. Remember the old saw that "rules are made to be broken"? They can also be bent or circumvented through loopholes. Executives, in many instances abetted—or at least not deterred—by their accountants, have taken full advantage of GAAP to increase their reporting flexibility, to manage earnings, and to report growth where none existed. It is not a coincidence that the first line of defenses for every question about accounting starts with "it conformed with GAAP" ignoring whether "it" was misleading or an outright lie.

Technology
Technology by nature is complex, and most nontechnicians, including those who sit on boards, have limited understanding of it. It's one thing for directors to grasp the meaning of a tangible product they can see and count. The task becomes infinitely more difficult when products are too small to be seen or when they do things beyond the comprehension of most people. This creates a dilemma for directors. How can they validate strategy and fulfill a checks and balances role if they can't understand the company's business model or its competitive environment, value drivers, and products and services?

Intangibles
It seems like ages since companies were valued for the most part by the assets they held. Today many of the world's largest companies are valued for their intangible assets—their brands, technologies, patents, and intellectual capital. While recent rulings that no longer require the amortization of intangible assets make sense, investors must realize that the periodic revaluation of intangibles will result in large and sudden changes in asset values and equity values. Directors cannot do their job unless they understand the factors that might result in a revaluation of intangible assets.

Mergers and Acquisitions
Mergers and acquisitions add a highly dynamic element to corporate structure, physical locations, accounting control practices,

asset definitions, and GAAP interpretations. Even if directors could get completely up-to-speed on a company's operations, each new acquisition would require them to gain new knowledge and understanding. Staying current with even a modest number of acquisitions is a formidable task. It becomes virtually impossible in companies that constantly merge and acquire.

The Disenfranchisement of Shareholders

BOARDS OF DIRECTORS were established because a large and dispersed group of shareholders simply cannot provide the kind of management oversight required to protect their own interests. Shareholders trust boards of directors to do that for them. If shareholders don't like what's happening in a company, the most effective direct action they can take is to sell the stock. To exert this power, however, individual shareholders must have complete and accurate information on the company's performance, which requires transparency on the part of the company.

Recently, CEOs and investor relations managers have often been heard congratulating themselves publicly for delivering more information and for "increasing transparency." And they are quick to point to their compliance with Regulation Full Disclosure, passed by the SEC in August 2000, which requires companies to release financial performance information to everyone simultaneously and theoretically gives investors equal opportunity to buy and sell shares on a timely basis. Undoubtedly, some companies are providing more detailed information to all people at the same time, but true transparency is both an absolute and a relative measure.

The complexity of the modern corporation has increased the level of difficulty for investors to understand and analyze the information they are given. As companies become more complex, investors need more information to understand them and to compare and contrast their operations and prospects. While more information may be disclosed now than several years ago, the investor's need for detailed information has outpaced the rate at which it is being provided and investors' ability to analyze it has diminished. Consequently, investors know less today than ever before of what they need to know to make intelligent capital allocation decisions.

Spinning the Story

With the help of public relations departments, CEOs have learned how to use print and broadcast media to spin their stories broadly in enticing sound bites, without a lot of supporting evidence or qualifying explanation. A day does not go by when a TV or radio financial show host doesn't ask a CEO what he is going to do to raise the company's stock price. Investors are treated to frequent personal appearances by CEOs explaining what a great job they are doing. Broadcasters eagerly anticipate quarterly earnings with countdowns to the announcement.

Sell-side analysts do not fare so well. The leading financial network routinely jabs sell-side researchers for moving as a group long after the horse has left the barn (or the share price as declined precipitously). Nonetheless, investors are still barraged with one-sided, self-serving research reports, effectively paid for by companies' CEOs through investment banking fees.

Where does that all leave the individual investors? Complexity has certainly inhibited their ability to gain a complete understanding of a company's overall performance. They can't rely on CEOs for transparency. And they certainly can't look to sell-side research for accurate, reliable analysis. Little wonder then that investors have found themselves hobbled and totally unable to vote with their feet in any informed or meaningful way.

Ineffectiveness of Proxy Contests

The legal and capital market system provides investors an alternative to voting with their feet to force good governance. Through a proxy contest, shareholders can propose a new slate of directors (and indirectly, management) when they feel that a company is not being managed for the investors' benefit. Such contests, unfortunately, are very expensive and often fail because institutional investors are reluctant to vote against the incumbent management and because few shareholders stand to gain more from a proxy contest than they would from selling their shares.

Lack of Institutional Leadership

Professional portfolio managers for pension funds, mutual funds, life insurance companies, and the like control more than 55 percent of equity securities.[9] These firms have large research departments to analyze not only the information reported by the companies, but also, and more important, information available from other independent sources. As fiduciaries for the individual investors in these funds, these professional managers control large amounts of stock and consequently have access to and some degree of influence over management. One might expect that such managers would be their investors' advocates for better governance of the companies in which their funds hold stock. And, in the absence of good governance, one might hope that fund managers would vote with their feet by selling their shares in those companies that fail to provide good information, cook the books, or are significantly overvalued because of the demand for "hot" stocks. They have not done so.

Even armed with better information and better analysis, professional portfolio managers are, after all, human. They are influenced by the same emotions as individual investors. Like individual investors, they can fall prey to the Greater Fool Theory. While they don't put their own capital on the line, their reputations are at stake.

To compound their woes, institutional investors, unlike individual investors, legitimately need to hold the stocks of large companies, many of which have been the most active players in the Share Price Game. Institutional investors benchmark their performance against the large indices, which include these large companies' stocks. They must, therefore, almost certainly hold those stocks in order to hedge performance. While institutional investors must hold onto large companies, they also cannot sell stock in small companies without incurring large costs because of the limited liquidity of such stocks. The frictional cost of self-induced declines in share price as the wholesale selling commences makes getting out very costly. Professional investors seldom vote with their feet until it's too late.

Institutional investors, unlike individual investors, need to hold the stocks of large companies, many of which have been the most active players in the Share Price Game.

A conflict in fiduciary responsibilities. Many professional fund managers, while shouldering a fiduciary responsibility to their investors, collect assets (the money they're paid to manage) from the pension funds of the public companies they buy and sell on behalf of their investors. Supposedly, the pension funds are separately managed, meaning that their decisions to allocate money to specific professional managers is not influenced by whether that manager has sold the company's stock. Few believe this to be true. Revenues of professional managers are most closely linked in the short term to the amount of money under management. Investment performance affects that amount over a longer time frame. The temptation to make decisions to attract or keep more money today at the possible cost of future performance is very great. For these money managers, revenue today affects their compensation today.

Companies that self-manage their pension funds create a conflict by ignoring the separation between the fiduciary obligation of the pension fund to employees and the desire of the CEO to manage stock price. The pension fund of one company routinely buys or sells the stock of another company and visa versa. Robert Monks, a well-respected shareholder advocate says, "It is the ugly not-so-secret reality that corporate pension funds are operating contrary to the law. The CEO of one company says to the CEO of another, 'My pension fund will not raise questions about your company if your pension fund will not raise questions about my company.' They have neutered themselves intentionally."[10]

Finally, as financial assets were allocated toward equities during the 1990s based on the expectation of extraordinary future equity returns, professional managers had to buy equities. Remember when "funds flows" explained daily advances in the market? Pension funds adopted revised guidelines that required a greater percentage of assets to be invested in equities. Managers were the victims of the momentum and of the bubble that they failed to prevent. Even as stocks declined, fund managers were further victimized. As equity prices fell, managers found they did not have enough marked-to-market value in equities to meet their own investment guidelines and were forced by their own rules to buy equities even though they realized that prices might still be overvalued. Some argue that this cushioned the fall but prolonged the problem.

Protecting against poor governance. Encouraging good governance is not only in the interest of professional investors, it is also their obligation as participants in the economic system. Otherwise, capital allocation is a crapshoot. Many institutional investors do not see things this way. They argue that as fiduciaries of individual investors, their job is to get it right—to buy low and sell high. Implicitly they make the case that better information and analysis in a large professional organization—especially theirs—provides an advantage in a competitive marketplace. Either they dismiss the argument that they are fiduciaries for both current and potential future investors or they argue that they are so smart that they consistently "get it right."

If these institutional investors were not conflicted, could realistically sell their large-cap stocks, and had the liquidity to sell mid-cap and small-cap stocks without excessive frictional losses, then their argument might be worth debating. What they can assert rightly is that their fiduciary responsibilities differ in material ways from those of corporate directors. The primary difference, however, is that while directors are responsible for providing accurate information, institutional investors are responsible for analyzing information thoroughly. Given investors' lack of will—much less their inability—to "vote with their feet," professional investors have a duty to protect against poor governance. Doing so is integral to achieving acceptable long-term performance.

Undoubtedly, monitoring and assessing governance will increase costs for professional investors. So will the SEC's new requirement that mutual funds tell investors how they vote on proxy issues. Mutual funds loudly

Executives of the companies in which money managers invest can already see how the funds vote on proxies, but the shareholders whose money funds control can't.

opposed the SEC's requirement. While voting proxies is clearly their obligation, they argued that voting, like stock picking and timing their buying and selling, is part of the investment process and that disclosure could harm their competitive advantage. Missing from the argument was any mention of the fact that management of the companies in which they invest already can see how the funds vote, but the shareholders whose money they control can't. The fund managers also pointed out that disclosure would burden them with significant additional costs that would harm their clients because the costs, of course, will be passed on to investors. With disclosure, however, investors can see more clearly how the funds are functioning as fiduciaries and decide for themselves if professional management is worth the price tag.

Antitakeover Initiatives

One school of thought says that the market itself will punish companies with poor governance practices. Those who take that position contend that companies with bad strategies, poor execution, or self-serving management will be forced to sell to better managed companies as shareholders revolt and tender their shares in a takeover. In the mid 1980s, more than half of the 100 largest companies in the United States were subject to tender offers.

As the takeover boom gained momentum, many argued for maintaining the status quo, mostly those who wanted to protect local business and jobs, and by extension the entrenched management of the underperforming enterprises. The Business Roundtable, composed of leading CEOs of the time, essentially took the position that the only good takeover is a dead takeover.

Lawmakers—lobbied by corporate lawyers and blue-chip CEOs—began passing rigorous laws making takeovers far more difficult and very expensive. The average tender offer in the 1980s was at a 40 percent premium over the current unaffected stock price. Then legislation was passed in Washington making unfriendly takeovers much more difficult; today most takeovers have to be of the more "friendly" variety, and the premium that goes to shareholders has shrunk considerably. To win a friendly deal, acquirers now pay a good deal of the premium to the management of a takeover target through golden parachutes, buy-outs, and special compensation deals. This isn't an argument for the return of unfriendly, surprise tender offers. Rather, it's one for directors to ensure that shareholders instead of management benefit from the premium paid in acquisitions.

In the 1980s Washington "fixed" the problem, and management became even more entrenched. If companies continue to play the Share Price Game, and directors continue to look the other way, Washington is likely to "fix" it again with even more legislation, the consequences of which are unpredictable.

Time to Restore Balance

THERE'S PLENTY OF BLAME to spread all around for the dramatic shift in the balance of power between management and boards of directors. Executives had the opportunity, incentives, and ability to grab power. Many boards became their willing cohorts, looked the other way, or allowed the shift of power to happen through benign neglect. Investors of all varieties failed to assert their will out of fear or greed.

Plenty of people have now stepped forward to try to put in the fix. Legislators and regulators are primed to take on the job, and certainly laws and regulations can help. The ultimate fix is up to boards of directors. They must reassert their power and accept fully their responsibilities and obligation to protect shareholders' interests. How they can do this is the subject of the next two chapters.

CHAPTER 7 # The Measure of a Board

THE CORPORATE GOVERNANCE CRISIS, post-Enron, is not the first in American history, but it may be the worst. The good news is that some believe we're past the most appalling part of it. No less an authority than Federal Reserve Board Chairman Alan Greenspan declared in testimony before the U.S. Congress on February 11, 2003, he doubted that any severe governance problems will have occurred after the summer of 2002, although some may come to light after that point. Certainly, on balance, there has been a pause in abuse.

The bad news is that this is not the first time that such declarations of victory have been voiced. In the late 1990s, just as the Share Price Game and compensation excesses were gaining real momentum, governance experts were assuring the investing public that real reform had already occurred. This view was reported broadly. *Business Week* noted in a November 1996 article, "Somehow, directors forgot—if they ever knew—that they were in the boardroom to act on behalf of shareholders and oversee that collection of hired hands known as management." The writer promptly assured readers that governance was improving: "Slowly but surely, however, a quiet revolution is going on in America's boardrooms. The directors around the conference table are waking up. They're taking the job more seriously."[1]

A year later, in 1997, *Business Week* declared that the war on poor governance had been won: "Not long ago ... In the clubby, cozy world that typified the corporate boardroom, CEOs packed their boards with trusted

A Conference Board survey reported that the boards of midsized companies actually devoted more time than those of large complex companies.

friends and colleagues who rarely challenged the chieftain's policies—or prerogatives.... Today, however, all that has changed."[2]

At the beginning of 2000, *Business Week* again assured readers that large companies had good governance, but noted that hundreds of midsized companies lacked independent boards. James E. Heard, chairman of Proxy Monitor, was quoted as saying, "With the exception of a few rogues, most boards are doing the job they are supposed to do." The *Business Week* article went on to say, "If the governance battle has largely been won at big companies, however the war is hardly over. Now the attention is shifting toward midsized and smaller companies."[3]

For several years, with earnings manufacture in full swing and the bursting of the dot-com bubble, this view was substantiated. Then came Enron, WorldCom, Xerox, Adelphia Communications, CMS Energy, Computer Associates, Applied Digital Solutions, Global Crossing, Halliburton, Lucent Technologies, Merck, Microsoft, Peregrine Systems, Qwest Communications, Rite Aid, AOL Time Warner, Squibb, Duke Energy, Kmart, Miriant, Tyco International, Williams Companies, Kimberly Clark, El Paso, Supervalu, Reliant Resources, Rayovac, Qualcomm Inc., Dynegy, and HealthSouth. All made the news with allegations against them of accounting irregularities. In October 2002, *Business Week* backpedaled temporarily, noting that a "wake-up call has spurred companies to make radical improvements. Problems that were simply ignored a couple of years ago are now the subject of heated boardroom debate."[4]

One month later, *Business Week* reported that many companies continued to report results in "the gray areas."[5] Two of the reported examples included Citigroup's doubling of its reported growth rate by counting a one-time gain on the sale of real estate as part of core earnings, and IBM's written earnings announcement failing to disclose that more than half of the improvement in earnings from the prior year also resulted from real estate gains. (When this failure to disclose was subsequently made public, an IBM spokesperson said, "We pride ourselves on straight talk to investors.") The authors of the *Business Week* article rightly concluded, "The new SEC rules should help clean up numbers some more. But they won't stop every executive from playing the gray areas of accounting judgments. If executives will spin numbers in this environment, they will in any. Investors will always need to look out for themselves."

According to a Conference Board survey of 660 companies,[6] in 2001 the median board met six times annually and the meetings lasted between three and four hours. This comes to a total of between eighteen to twenty-four hours annually. The survey also reported that the boards of midsized companies (annual revenues of approximately $1 billion) actually spent more time than those of large complex companies that had more than $10 billion in annual revenues. No doubt, in the wake of recent scandals, directors are spending more time preparing for and sitting in board meetings. But is it enough, given the manifold increase in corporate complexity and the myriad issues that boards face today?

The Ineffectiveness
of Governance Guidelines

IN A BROADLY BASED RESPONSE to the crisis, the New York Stock Exchange, Nasdaq, The Conference Board, The National Association of Corporate Directors, and various governance rating services have all issued best practices guidelines. Governance experts have used them as a measure of improved performance by boards of directors. All of these organizations made good-faith efforts to improve corporate governance. Failure to abide by the guidelines issued by the major stock exchanges, for example, could result in a company losing its listing. Those issued by the prestigious Conference Board, on the other hand, rely solely on logical suasion to encourage reform. In either case, shareholders should feel grateful that new guidelines have caused executives, directors, and the investing public to think harder about what good governance actually means. Unfortunately, the benefits of these guidelines may stop there. In truth, a board may comply with all these suggestions and continue to perform poorly.

If Sarbanes-Oxley had been passed in the 1990s, would it have prevented the abuses and scandals of the past few years? The evidence seems to point to no.

The ineffectiveness to promote real change may stem from how the guidelines were developed. The issuers of guidelines usually solicit input from corporate executives and other interested parties, all of whom may have conflicting interests. It's a familiar process. Someone proposes a fairly radical new rule that will strongly encourage or even force change. Then the howls of protest begin. Those affected, the companies and lobbyists alike, point out real as well as obscure unintended consequences as they attempt to protect their own interests. The meaningful change morphs into the most benign change possible.

Most of these guidelines are at best quite bland: Require an independent director to approve CEO compensation. Have a majority of independent directors on the board (after a grace period). Adopt a written code of corporate conduct. Have a written charter for the audit and other committees. Require the audit committee chairperson to know something about finance. Require CEO certification of financial statements. Gain stockholder approval of equity-based compensation plans. Hardly anyone would argue with the appropriateness of any of those guidelines; they're commonsense rules. And few boards, if any, would have a terribly difficult time complying with them.

Boards wanting compliance assistance, however, will find it readily available. Some rating services not only publish guidelines and rate companies on compliance, they also provide consulting services and canned solutions to help boards achieve compliance. Jeffrey Sonnenfeld, Associate Dean of the Yale School of management described such practices in a *Wall Street Journal* article titled, "Introducing the Watchdogs for Corporate Governance." He noted that if companies purchase accredited director training and consulting services to evaluate director incentive packages from the rating agency Institutional Shareholder Service, "the client's payoff is a nice boost in scores."[7] At least it's an efficient process: one stop shopping for better governance.

Guidelines are checklists, and checking the boxes has little or nothing to do with good governance. By checking the right boxes, companies can give the appearance of improved governance; some may believe they actually have improved. But by-the-numbers conformance to guidelines, in and of itself, does not prevent terrible governance.

The Inadequacy of Government Legislation

THE SARBANES-OXLEY ACT OF 2002 has been hailed as the legislation that will restore public confidence in corporate America and the capital markets. Unfortunately, it will probably have little more lasting impact on actually improving governance than will guidelines.

According to a PricewaterhouseCoopers Management Barometer survey, only about one-third of executives surveyed believe that Sarbanes-Oxley will restore confidence in the capital markets or aid their companies' ability to create shareholder value. Only 9 percent of executives characterized it as a good and adequate response to problems in accounting and reporting.[8] Not to paint too dark a picture, the legislation does hold forth some potential benefits. The act calls for establishing the Public Company Accounting Oversight Board with authority to impose penalties for violation of its rules.

If its leaders are committed to real change, this new Board could have a significant and meaningful effect on corporate governance practices. Under the law, the Board has the authority to change the interpretation of GAAP to tighten loopholes, to eliminate special interest exemptions, and to move GAAP away from a rules-based toward a more

With the exception of making loans to selected officers, Enron appears to have been in substantial compliance with Sarbanes-Oxley at the time of its catastrophic fall.

principles-based system. This prospect would certainly terrify anyone who has manufactured earnings or benefited from them. It might also be of special concern to managers and directors who would then be unable to fall back on the "it conforms with GAAP" defense. Unless the new Board uses its powers well, with the appropriate degree of proof of culpability, its ability to impose and enforce penalties will quickly diminish.

Other Sarbanes-Oxley provisions have generated a lot of press, but in reality represent only marginal changes and benefits. For example, the benefit of the provision requiring that CEOs personally certify financial statements is primarily psychological. In truth, they've always had that responsibility. Perhaps now they will take it a bit more seriously. (A drawback of this provision is that it tends to let directors off the hook; many directors believed that they and the CEO already certified the financial statements when they submitted a Form 10K SEC filing.)

Much of Sarbanes-Oxley deals with separating financial auditing from management consulting and with addressing conflicts of interest or inappropriate relationships among corporate financial officers and their independent auditing firms. Those are important, but shouldn't directors have been sufficiently diligent to address such obvious issues without the hammer of legislation? Debating that point is of little use; the legislation is sufficiently loose that abuses and problems will most likely continue. The act also attempts to recoup from CEOs any incentive income they earned within a year of having issued misleading financial statements or within a year of material reporting irregularities. If the income falls outside of the one-year limit, the CEO gets to keep the money, which weakens this provision significantly.

If Sarbanes-Oxley had been passed in the 1990s, would it have prevented the abuses and scandals of the past few years? The evidence seems to point to "no." With the exception of making loans to selected officers, Enron appears to have been in substantial compliance with the corporate responsibility provisions of Sarbanes-Oxley at the time of its catastrophic fall.

A Wonderful World of Governance

The Walt Disney Company has been criticized widely for its poor governance practices. The basic complaint is that CEO and board chairman Michael Eisner has the company's directors in his pocket, and the board is not independent. That said, several directors, Stanley Gold (CEO of Shamrock Capital Partners) in particular, have challenged Eisner on the company's poor performance and high pay package. Most likely in response to pressure from the press and governance experts, Disney has said that it is taking steps to improve governance. A careful analysis, however, reveals that these are less than giant steps.

The board, chaired by Eisner, met on December 3, 2002, and announced that it had adopted a stricter definition of independence, consistent with NYSE guidelines. As a result, Stanley Gold, whose daughter worked for Disney, was disqualified as an independent director, making it impossible for him to serve on key committees including the governance and nominating, audit, and compensation committees. At about the same time, Disney cancelled contracts with two other board members, former U.S. Senator George Mitchell, whose law firm provided legal services to Disney, and architect Robert Stern. While Gold, the dissenter, was disqualified as an independent director, Mitchell and Stern maintained their "independence" because their contracts had been cancelled.[9]

Eisner then announced that he favored the appointment of a "presiding director" who would chair at least two board meetings annually, at which Eisner and management would not be present. Eisner also hired Ira Millstein, a respected lawyer who has served on several Blue Ribbon Commissions on governance, which bolstered the perception of good governance at Disney. Millstein noted that many companies were appointing lead directors or even separating the role of board chairman and company president/CEO. The implication was that Disney's move was consistent with such good governance.

How did this play out in practice? Whether the individual is called "lead director" or "presiding director," he or she has only as much power as they can assume or as the CEO allows. In Disney's case, Eisner continued to serve as both chairman of the board and CEO. Eisner appointed Mitchell to the position of "presiding director." Obviously intelligent and certainly well-respected, Mitchell comes with great credentials. What he doesn't come with is an abundance of time to devote to the job. Mitchell serves on a total of eight boards, sits on ten important subcommittees of those boards, and is chairman of four of the committees—all while being a practicing lawyer. This is the man who is expected to identify issues, collect and analyze information, lead discussions on relevant issues, and based on those discussions, maintain a meaningful dialogue with management and foster a checks and balances culture.

At about the same time that Disney was touting its new and improved governance, more information about the company's disclosure practices and director independence came to light. In its annual report filed in December 2002, the company confirmed two previously undisclosed items: (1) It paid more than $600,000 to a company affiliated with a director for use of a private plane; (2) It gave $20 million and pledged an additional $5 million to a charity whose CEO later became a Disney director. Spinning these facts as fast as possible, Millstein noted that in most cases these disclosures were not required and said, "As long as you tell everybody what you're doing, that's good governance,"[10]

a position with which investors who claim no governance expertise at all might take issue.

Good Governance Takes More

Jeffrey Sonnenfeld in a *Harvard Business Review* article titled
"What Makes Great Boards Great,"[11] says that, by definition,
guidelines and checklists address structural issues such as board
composition, board size, age of directors, number of meetings,
number of meetings without
management, existence of committees, powers of various committees, and definitions of
independence. He points out,
however, that what determines
the quality of governance is
"not rules and regulations, it's
the way people work together."

> *Duty of loyalty, as defined by Monks and Minow, requires directors to "demonstrate unyielding loyalty to the company's shareholders."*

In other words, social and cultural issues, not strict adherence to
guidelines and checklists, are the differentiating factors between
good and poor governance. Sonnenfeld also maintains that
almost no correlation exists between good governance and such
characteristics as the age of board members, their independence
(as defined by Sarbanes-Oxley), the size of the board, and committee structures.

Rules and regulations do not force directors to think independently, nor do they assure that directors have sufficient
understanding of an issue to make a well-reasoned decision.
Some regulations and guidelines attempt to define independence in concrete terms. Others are designed to give directors an
opportunity to confer among themselves in committee or executive sessions. None of these guidelines can ensure that directors
understand the details of the business sufficiently well to raise the
right questions. Similarly, requiring boards to spend more time,
hold more meetings, or form more committees in no way ensures
that directors are actually attempting to do a good job.

Regulations containing penalties for failure to exercise duty of care or duty of loyalty, discussed in detail in the next few pages, are not much more effective. The burden of proof for criminal or even civil penalties should be high. The SEC has prosecuted takeover professionals and some Wall Street types, but very few directors have been prosecuted, and the threat of punishment appears not to be an overwhelming deterrent.

Two Duties of Directors

IT IS GENERALLY AGREED that directors on corporate boards must meet two standards in order to fulfill their fiduciary obligations to shareholders. The two standards are called "duty of loyalty" and "duty of care."

Duty of loyalty, as defined by Monks and Minow, requires directors to "demonstrate unyielding loyalty to the company's shareholders."[12] Because one of the primary responsibilities of directors is to protect shareholders from potential agency issues—management's disregard for shareholder interests or, worse, overriding self-interest for personal gain—a prerequisite for duty of loyalty is for directors to be independent of undue influence by management in their oversight and decision-making responsibilities.

The second standard, duty of care, requires directors "to exercise due diligence" in making decisions. In other words, they must discover as much information as reasonably possible on the issues they face and be able to show that in reaching a decision they have considered all reasonable alternatives.[13] In assessing the conduct of directors, the courts rely on the "business judgment rule," which holds that if directors make decisions based on their loyalty to shareholders and to the company (instead of to management) and act with care, it is assumed that they have used their best judgment and are not liable for their decisions.

In short, duty of loyalty assures that directors want to do what's in the best interest of shareholders. Duty of care requires that they spend the time and resources to do it diligently. The business judgment rule says that they must want to and try to do the

right thing it, but they can be wrong. They may make bad decisions, but will have done so in good faith to shareholders and for
defensible reasons. This does not seem like a particularly bur-
densome requirement.

One specific re-
quirement for directors
to demonstrate their
duty of loyalty has
remained relatively con-
sistent over time: Dir-
ectors cannot self-deal.
In other words, as fidu-

**Duty of care requires directors
"to exercise due diligence"
in making decisions. In other
words, they must discover as
much information as reasonably
possible on the issues.**

ciaries they cannot make decisions for their personal gain. In 1861
a judge in New York observed, "No principle is better settled than
that a person having a duty to perform for others cannot act in
the same matter for his own benefit."[14]

This narrow interpretation of duty of loyalty does not address
the agency problem at all, and only covers one potential conflict
of loyalty. It specifies "who" directors *will not* favor—themselves,
but it does not specify "who" they *will* favor—shareholders
instead of management. Although duty of loyalty has been so narrowly—some would argue sloppily—defined, the courts have
consistently held that duty of loyalty imposes far broader requirements than simply avoiding self-dealing.

The purpose of duty of care is to ensure that directors know
and understand what is going on in their companies. Although
the concept of duty of care has existed since the 1700s, the interpretation of exactly how much "care" directors must exercise has
fluctuated over time. If anything, the interpretation has become
more lenient as the tasks of oversight and strategy approval have
become more difficult. A good part of the difficulty stems from
the increasing complexity of companies. Regulations and guidelines have proven ineffective in motivating directors to exercise
greater diligence. And the exercise of true independence has
been thwarted by the alignment of executive and director interests in opposition to the long-term interests of shareholders (as

Simply put, faced with a greater need for care, directors have successfully argued for more lenient tests of their accountability instead of increasing diligence.

described in Chapter 2). Simply put, faced with a greater need for care, directors have successfully argued for more lenient tests of their accountability instead of increasing diligence.

This is particularly troublesome because protection has never been more important, and shareholders are less able than ever to look out for themselves. They have become a larger and more dispersed group. They can't sell as easily now when they see deteriorating performance or other signs of company distress. They can't oust those responsible, specifically executive management or board members. It seems abundantly clear the only mechanism that can truly protect investors' interests is for directors to adhere to the highest standards of duty of care and duty of loyalty.

Duty of Loyalty

AS NOTED EARLIER, a prerequisite for duty of loyalty is for directors to be independent, not influenced by either friendship with, moral obligations to, or fear of dismissal by management. Directors can be friends of management as long as both parties understand and expect that the director's fiduciary obligation to shareholders will outweigh friendship. Independence can be compromised if directors as much as suspect that they are obligated to management for their seat on the board. Many directors need the compensation they receive. If keeping their jobs depends on keeping management happy, they will not be able to execute their fiduciary responsibilities to shareholders.

Two conditions must exist for an entire board of directors to meet the duty of loyalty standards. The first is an independent state of mind, reinforced by meaningful rules that hopefully increase the probability of independence. The second condition is that a majority of a board's directors come from outside the

company and not from the company's executive management
team. These two conditions are interrelated. With more rigorous
standards of independence, a simple majority of independent
directors will be more likely to assure duty of loyalty for the whole
board. With lower standards, a greater majority is needed to
counterbalance a director or directors who do not exhibit independence on a given issue.

Exercising duty of loyalty without at least a majority of independent directors is very difficult. In recognition of that, the New York
Stock Exchange and Nasdaq guidelines recently required a majority of independent directors on the boards of listed companies,
whereas Sarbanes-Oxley was silent on the matter of board makeup.

Defining Independence

The legal definition of independence, as found in the Sarbanes-
Oxley Act of 2002, is perhaps the narrowest interpretation of
independence that could have been written. It fails to address
many, if not most, of the most critical issues that affect duty of loyalty. According to Sarbanes-Oxley, independence means "not
receiving, other than for service on the board, any consulting,
advisory, or other compensatory fee from the issuer, and as not
being an affiliated person of the issuer, or any subsidiary thereof."
In other words, according to this act, independence means not
being paid directly or specially and not being a member of management. It ignores the real-life issues that might cause directors
to put management's interests ahead of shareholder, including:

- friendships with the CEO or other senior executives
- appointment to and continued service on the board, with its
  prestige and compensation at the pleasure of the CEO
- being CEOs themselves and therefore having a viewpoint sym-
  pathetic to that of management
- being part of interlocking directorships

**Independence according to the National Association of Corporate
Directors.** The Blue Ribbon Commission (BRC) on Audit
Committees of the National Association of Corporate Directors

articulated a more detailed and marginally better definition of independence in its 2000 report. This definition says that a director will be considered independent if he or she:

● has not been an employee of the corporation or any of its subsidiaries within the last five years
● is not a close relative of any management-level employee of the company
● provides no significant services or goods to the company
● is not employed by any firm providing major services to the company, and
● receives no significant compensation from the company, other than director's fee[15]

The BRC notes that its definition is modeled after one previously published in the 1994 Report of the Blue Ribbon Commission on Performance Evaluation of Chief Executive Officers, Boards, and Directors. This means that the definition of independence, similar to Sarbanes-Oxley, has, for a decade, ignored many of the same real-life factors that can affect a director's ability to demonstrate true independence from management.

Independence according to The Business Roundtable. The membership of The Business Roundtable consists of CEOs of the 150 largest U.S. companies. Although this group has been criticized for procrastinating on governance issues in the past, they have, to their credit, developed one of the more thoughtful definitions of director independence. Certainly the CEOs of the largest companies in America should be well aware of all the factors that might make independent directors behave less independently. They should be applauded for taking a position that supports greater independence. The test will be whether or not they practice what they preach.

The Business Roundtable includes this in the discussion of independence in its white paper, "Principles of Corporate Governance," published in May 2002: "A substantial majority of directors of the board of a publicly owned corporation should be independent of management, both in fact and appearance, as determined by the board" and that an independent director should be "free of any relationship with the corporation or its management that may impair, or appear to impair, the director's ability to make independent judgments."

The publication references the listing standards of the major securities markets as "useful guidance in determining whether a particular director is 'independent.'" It also says that boards should consider whether "close personal relationships between potential board members and senior management might affect a director's actual or perceived independence."[16]

> *For an entire board of directors to meet the duty of loyalty standards, the majority must come from outside the company and not from the company's executive suite.*

Practicing Independence

This Business Roundtable definition sounds good, but can boards live by it? Many boards declare through a vote that individual directors are independent, even if there are indications that they might not be. For example, many directors who provide services to the company and are paid directly or indirectly for those services have been declared independent. While a board may declare a director to be independent, shareholders should be able to judge for themselves if the board's declaration is reasonable. They can't do that if they don't know which qualities the boards considered in making its determination. If individual directors must disclose to the board information that might call their independence into question, shouldn't boards then disclose that information to investors? Better yet, shouldn't boards explain to shareholders why they have deemed a director independent?

In their 1932 classic, *The Modern Corporation & Private Property,* Adolf Berle and Gardiner Means articulated this concept of disclosure:

The one ethical point on which everyone is agreed is that the adverse interest, if any, must be disclosed. There appears to be a general feeling that where a man represents adverse interests without letting that fact be known, he has created a situation so dangerous as not to be tolerated in the business community.[17]

Although this basic concept seems to have fallen by the wayside, it sounds like a sensible position for the business community and for directors in particular to take today.

From Russia With Independence

Understandably, changes to governance standards in the United States, including a reasonable definition of independence, have tended to be incremental. Interestingly, the Russian government has issued the most comprehensive and specific definition of independence by basically starting from scratch. The definition (see **FIGURE 7-1**) was part of an effort to demonstrate good governance in Russia to enable Russian companies to be listed on the London stock exchange. According to the Investor Protection Association, the definition was developed, based "on recommendations of international financial institutions, major Russian and foreign investors and issuers."[18] Being the most comprehensive does not necessarily make it the ultimate definition, but at least it candidly describes the many issues that could impact independence.

Duty of Care

IN 1742 THE STANDARD OF "CARE" as distinct from the standard of "loyalty" was clear. Speaking about corporate directors, the English Lord Chancellor said, "By accepting a trust of this sort, a person is obliged to execute it with fidelity and reasonable diligence; and it is no excuse to say that they had no benefit from it, but that it was merely honorary."[19] In 1880, in the case of *Hun v. Cary*,[20] Justice Earl interpreted "fidelity and reasonable diligence" to mean that a director "possesses at least ordinary knowledge and skill, and that he will bring them to bear in the discharge of his duties."

F I G U R E   7 - 1
Defining Independence in Russia

An Independent Director:

1. Is not financially or otherwise depending on the company's management, controlling (dominating) shareholders, large counterparts, and competitors

2. Is not a representative of the state

3. Is not at the same time a member of the executive body

4. Is not financially or otherwise depending on the company's affiliated persons (owners of 20 percent or more votes, members of the Board of Directors, auditor, ...)

5. Does not represent consultants contracted by the company

6. Has publicly declared his Independent Director status

7. Receives the remuneration for his work at the Board of Directors only from the company

8. Has necessary qualifications

9. Works faithfully in the BoD

10. Has a good reputation

11. Disseminates accurate information about the company and maximally facilitates to disseminate access to information by all shareholders of the company

12. Personal transactions of the director and his relatives with the company's shares (and other financial instruments) are transparent for the company and its shareholders

13. In case, if the Independent Director stops meeting the requirements of the Independent Director Status during his work at the Board of Directors, he immediately informs the company about this

14. The Independent Director agrees to disseminate the information about material facts to shareholders upon their request, in case, if the company did not disseminate such information in a legally defined time period

Directors at that time agreed wholeheartedly that this relatively benign standard was appropriate. Even though they wanted everyone to understand that they served because of their particular wisdom and knowledge, they felt that they should not be held to a higher than average standard of care. They claimed that if they exercised duty of loyalty that they could not be held liable except for "gross" negligence or inattention to duty. This claim is eerily similar and has obvious parallels to the "plausible deniability" arguments that have been used to defend directors much more recently.

In the 1873 case of *Railroad Co. v. Lockwood,* the U.S. Supreme Court overturned the theory that directors were liable for only "gross negligence" and not for "slight negligence."[21] In his opinion, Justice Joseph P. Bradley concluded that "negligence" means simply "failure to bestow the care and skill which the situation demands." Chief Justice Melville W. Fuller, in his comments, said that the "degree of care to which directors are bound is that which ordinarily prudent and diligent men would exercise under similar circumstances."[22]

Many directors and governance experts recently have expressed concern that directors simply will not serve if they will be held accountable to a higher standard of care. That argument isn't a new one. It's essentially the same as the argument put forth in the late nineteenth century, and described by Berle and Means, that the courts should be lenient in defining standards of care and in sentencing because requiring diligence of directors would prevent "gentlemen of property and means" from accepting directorships. Chief Justice Melvin W. Fuller's opinion at that time held differently: if "gentlemen of property and means" did not propose to run the business with care, they were not acceptable directors. It's hard not to compare the "gentlemen of property and means" of more than one hundred years ago with those who sit on today's boards of directors.

The Narrowing of Duty of Care

During the 1900s, as businesses became increasingly large and complex, boards of directors continued to press for a narrower interpretation of duty of care. As their job got harder, instead of working harder, directors thought the standards of performance should be lowered. In 1963 the Delaware Court of Chancery, ruling in *Graham v. Allis Chalmers Manufacturing Co.*,[23] supported and confirmed that the boards of directors of large, complex companies were merely a policy-making entity. Unless they became aware of early warning signs of trouble, they had no legal duty to actively provide a check-and-balance mechanism by establishing a legal compliance program. In

> **The Business Roundtable has, to its credit, developed one of the more thoughtful definitions of director independence.**

essence, this decision said that directors could assume that there was no agency problem unless it became obvious that there was one.

This opinion undoubtedly diluted duty of care standards by focusing narrowly on legal compliance rather than the broader issue of fiduciary responsibility. In 1996, however, the courts again reset duty of care standards. In a Caremark International, Inc. ruling, the Delaware Court's Chancellor William Allen substantially reversed the Graham decision by saying directors had to "exercise a good faith judgment that the corporation's information and reporting system is, in concept and design, adequate to assure the board that appropriate information will come to its attention in a timely manner as a matter of ordinary operations."

Today, the general belief is that to fulfill this standard, directors must continually ask probing questions and be skeptical. The majority view is definitely trending to the standard expressed by Chief Justice Bradley that duty of care requires "the care and skill that the situation demands." From a shareholder perspective, that is a reasonable expectation of directors. It's also reasonable that the standard espoused by Justice Bradley 120 years ago makes good sense today.

Many directors today, however, seem to reject the argument that they really need to understand the details of a business. By their actions they say that "ordinarily diligent and prudent men" need only attend a reasonable number of board meetings, rely solely on information supplied to them by the managers they oversee, and vote with the CEO after a few minutes of discussion. In light of the current state of governance, they may want to reevaluate this view.

Incremental Improvement Falls Short

Often when CEOs and directors take small steps toward better governance, it's hard to tell if they genuinely want to change their behavior or if they have simply realized that they must finally give a little ground. There is good reason to believe that many directors and executives only react to embarrassing disclosures, new compliance requirements, court rulings, or more stringent sentencing guidelines for negligence or fraud.

In the mid 1990s when victory over governance problems was declared, the practice of incremental improvements was labeled "governance by embarrassment."[24] More recently, Mike Mayo called it "just-in-time-governance" in reference to Sandy Weill and the board at Citigroup.[25] Criticized for questionable financing for Enron and WorldCom, spinning IPO shares, and biased research, Weill decided to expense options, established a governance committee, promised to avoid hidden off-balance-sheet structures, and later refused a cash bonus ostensibly because the stock price had declined by 25 percent. The board promptly granted him new options on 1.5 million shares of stock that experts valued at $17.9 million. As proof of his reformation, he was nominated as a director of the New York Stock Exchange, a nomination that was withdrawn after howls of protest.

There are many other examples of better governance by default. In 1991, when Federal Organizational Sentencing Guidelines said that companies with compliance programs and procedures would be subject to more lenient treatment than companies without them, boards suddenly leaped on the compliance program bandwagon. When regulations required that audit committees include members with financial expertise, boards started paying considerably more attention to this important qualification. When Sarbanes-Oxley required that CEOs sign off on the accuracy of financial statements, executives began asking their subordinates for assurance that the numbers were correct. When investors complained loudly about obviously excessive executive compensation, minor adjustments and givebacks were made.

Wouldn't such actions have been good practice in the absence of regulatory and legislative mandates, embarrassments, or threats of punishment? Obviously, regulation and legislation are needed to support better

Today, the general belief is that to fulfill the duty of care standard, directors must continually ask probing questions and be skeptical.

governance and higher standards. But that's not enough. Directors must accept that they now have a larger obligation to diligently exercise duty of loyalty and duty of care because other mechanisms that ought to protect investors' interests have been compromised.

CHAPTER 8 Principles of Good Governance

IN TOTAL, the three major stock exchanges in the United States list more than 8,500 publicly traded companies. Each company, of course, has its own corporate culture, operational challenges, competitive environment, and management and governance structures. It would be naïve to think that a single, finite set of rules, regardless of how well intentioned and comprehensive, could ever ensure good governance across the vast diversity of corporate America.

To begin with, governance already has its fair share of rules. How would you create new ones with enough specificity to govern the intangible, but critical, qualities of good governance—state of mind, diligence, ethics, honesty? It seems extremely daunting. And rules can always be gamed. Rules-based governance would be at least as easy to finesse as rules-based accounting.

New strictures would no doubt also come with a morass of additional unintended consequences. For example, requiring boards to have a financial expert on audit committees has created a class of directors that by definition are more knowledgeable than others in certain aspects of governance. Those less well-versed in financial matters may, as a result, consider themselves less accountable for the numbers. Proposals to separate the chairman and CEO roles may result in "chairmen" who have neither the time nor the insight to identify critical issues on a timely basis. On the investor side of the issue, the vast number of shareholders who are becoming increasingly disenchanted and frustrated with the ineffectiveness of current rules-based governance could decide to channel their capital away from U.S. equities rather than endure more of the same—or worse.

It's Not Rocket Science

CORPORATE GOVERNANCE is not a science subject to immutable rules. It is a culture of relationships. Whether or not it works depends on how its participants behave and interact with each other. Good governance comes from developing the right relationships among the right people. It requires that participants have the right information and knowledge as well as the incentives and ethics to do the right thing. Ensuring that all this happens falls squarely on the shoulders of those most closely involved and affected: directors, management, and shareholders. Their failure to shoulder the burden so far is underscored by the fact that rule-making groups have been so active of late.

Reform shouldn't focus on dictating behavior. Instead it needs to establish principles of good governance supported by mechanisms that stress accountability, disclosure, performance measurement, and checks and balances.

Chapter 5 discussed five cornerstones of principles-based accounting standards as put forth by DiPiazza and Eccles in *Building Public Trust: The Future of Corporate Reporting.* Borrowing from that concept, corporate governance principles should focus on the substance of directors' responsibilities and obligations: loyalty to shareholders and diligent care in oversight and decision making. As such, these principles of corporate governance should be built on five cornerstones:

- Address "state of mind" issues—attitude, accountability, integrity, ethics
- Adhere unfailingly to the substance of duty of loyalty and duty of care

- Articulate concepts applicable across all companies and industries
- Avoid rule setting that would allow exceptions and compromises to narrow principles
- Result in corporate governance that puts shareholders' interests first

A principles-based system of corporate governance relies on trust, depends on fiduciaries, and requires validation. Similar to the democratic form of government, principles-based governance benefits from scrutiny, debate, and, most of all, transparency. This chapter articulates the principles and conduct required to assure good corporate governance. Many may pay lip service to these principles but fail to live by them day to day.

Corporate governance is not a science subject to immutable rules. It is a culture of relationships.

The specific recommendations are extensions of the principles: what is required to establish and implement principles-based governance mechanisms and how management, boards, and investors can live the principles.

The principles and conduct described here are divided into two broad categories: (1) those addressing shareholder/board relationship issues and (2) those addressing board/management relationship issues. Within these categories are specific recommendations for shareholders, directors, and executives. To the extent that any of these recommendations approach the specificity of a guideline or a rule, it is because they are extensions of a principle that can apply to most, if not all, companies. Recognizing that one size can't fit all, mandating compliance by legislation and regulation is not the solution. Rather, boards of directors of specific companies must take the responsibility for implementing these recommendations, ensuring their adherence to the principles, and holding themselves accountable for their substance. Investors should judge them on how well they have done so and allocate capital to companies that can truly demonstrate that they live up to the principles of good governance in spirit and in action.

The Board/Shareholder Relationship

THE SARBANES-OXLEY ACT OF 2002 requires that CEOs and CFOs certify the accuracy of their companies' publicly reported financial statements with a "to the best of my knowledge" qualifier. When this requirement was under consideration in congressional committee, the drafters of the legislation at one point envisioned that directors would also certify financial statements with the same caveat. Following intense lobbying against that provision by John Snow, then Chairman of the Business Roundtable and now Secretary of the Treasury, this requirement was rejected. Snow and his supporters argued that directors could not have a sufficiently detailed grasp of the financials to fulfill the certification requirements. Frankly, the same could be argued of CEOs in large, complex organizations who rely on others to verify the numbers and demonstrate reasonable diligence when certifying.

If the CEO is willing to certify, and directors trust the CEO implicitly as they have proclaimed so often, why would directors not feel comfortable adding their own certification to the financial statements? Perhaps directors trust their CEOs only to the extent that they will not be held to a reasonable standard of diligence if the CEO just happens to be wrong.

Commit to Independence and Care

Even though directors don't have the CEO's responsibility to certify the financials, it seems at least reasonable to expect independent directors to commit to a comparable standard: to declare publicly that they will act independently (duty of loyalty) and will take the time and expend the effort (duty of care) required to exercise their responsibilities fully. Directors should make that public commitment by executing an oath of independence and care annually, with each board making its own determination about the content and degree of specificity of their oath.

Five cornerstones of good governance: adhere to duty of loyalty, honor duty of care, be consistent across all companies, avoid exceptions, put shareholders' interests first.

Such an oath would not be a promise to always be right, but it would be an oath to do what is right in good faith and to the best of the individual director's ability. Just as Sarbanes-Oxley did not impose any real additional burden of responsibility on CEOs and CFOs, an oath for directors would simply affirm that they understand their responsibilities completely and undertake fulfilling them with the utmost seriousness and honesty.

Ensure Transparency and Fair Disclosure

Investors have the choice of investing in multiple industries and thousands of companies within those industries. Most of the information investors receive about a company's performance comes from or is heavily influenced by management. With so much competition for their capital and so much information in the hands of management, why should investors ever have to expose themselves to risk because of poor or incomplete information?

Before investors make a decision, they should ask three questions: Why should they have confidence that a company's management and board of directors are focused on managing the business to create real value instead of managing stock price? Why should they trust the company to report the results of its performance with integrity and honesty? And what evidence do they have that management fully discloses the risks it takes to earn an acceptable return and to enable investors to determine whether future anticipated return justifies those risks?

One way shareholders can get answers those questions is to pose them to management and the board. Shareholders and prospective shareholders should reasonably expect that a company's management and board would be willing to tell them everything they need to know about the business to evaluate the soundness of their investments. This should exclude, of course, information that would compromise the competitive position of the business.

Management and boards constant-

Directors should make a public commitment by executing an oath of independence and care annually.

ly must make the trade-off between full disclosure with transparency and the need to preserve a competitive advantage.

Companies routinely choose to withhold information because they consider it immaterial. Clearly companies cannot disclose every detail. However, if investors feel that they need specific information because they consider it material, such as the impact of a group of secondary events, the burden should fall to companies to explain why they will not disclose information. If shareholders do not like the answer, they should choose another investment. The kind of information that is important to investors may differ markedly from that which is material to the company. For example, an undisclosed $10 million options benefit to an executive might not be material to a major company's earnings. It would, however, be quite relevant to the individual who received it. It might also be very significant to investors who have placed their trust in that individual and who rightly should expect the board to tell them how their money is being spent.

Investors who own securities directly and professional fund managers who serve as fiduciaries for many investors all share a certain degree of responsibility for ensuring good governance in the companies they own. The federal government is subject to the will of the electorate—its leaders serve at the pleasure of those who vote—and directors who bear responsibility for protecting shareholders' interests should be subject to their input.

Direct Lines of Communication

As fiduciaries for shareholders, boards have an obligation to communicate directly with them and to establish mechanisms that allow investors to have contact with them. For example, independent directors should meet at least once annually with institutional investors. These meetings should, of course, be webcast to comply with the Regulation Fair Disclosure act of 2001. At a minimum, a company's annual report and website should prominently display e-mail and postal addresses that shareholders can use to contact the board and individual directors.

The ability of investors to communicate directly with directors imposes an additional and considerable burden on board members. The Internet and e-mail have empowered individual shareholders to express their views more openly. Boards have voiced concern that if shareholders can contact its members individually, directors will be overburdened. Undoubtedly boards will have to sift through some less-than-constructive correspondence, but the benefit of knowing shareholders' views and pursuing constructive dialog will be worth the extra effort.

The board should have staff support (independent of management) and resources required to receive, evaluate and, if appropriate, respond to communications they receive from investors. Management should not screen communications or control the process. Their doing so would certainly compromise a healthy checks-and-balances system.

In practice, few companies provide mechanisms for direct communication between shareholders and directors. Some large pension funds, however, have taken steps to make shareholder feedback easier. The New York City Pension Funds, for example, have proposed that six of the companies it invests in establish offices with staff that report to a committee of independent directors to facilitate communication with investors.

A Meaningful Voice in Director Selection

In the United States, to be nominated for important elected government positions, candidates must first present their credentials and platforms to voters in primary elections. The winners of those primaries then run against other nominated candidates in a general election. The election process for boards of directors for corporations is different. A group of existing directors, the nominat-

In selecting directors, nominating committees should expand their candidate selection process beyond the CEO's handpicked slate.
ing committee, puts together the slate of candidates, usually with a great deal of input from the CEO. Almost always, a single candidate is nominated for each open position, and that predetermined slate is put forward to the shareholders for a vote.

This concept may not be fatally flawed. Nominating committees should, however, expand their candidate selection process beyond the CEO's handpicked slate. They should actively solicit input and suggestions from shareholders and others who have a stake in how the company is run. Boards should also explain in detail to shareholders why each candidate was nominated, what expertise the candidate brings to the job, and what makes the candidate truly independent.

The following hypothetical help-wanted ad could serve as a good blueprint for developing the criteria boards use for nominating directors and in explaining the candidates' appropriateness to investors. Nearly every characteristic described in this "want ad" has been endorsed by one or more better governance commissions or panels.

Help Wanted: Independent Director

Person independent of management influence willing and able to devote the time and effort required to collect, analyze and understand all reasonably available information with regard to the company, or to oversee such processes, to make informed and defensible business judgments in the best interests of all present and future potential shareholders. Highest integrity is mandatory.

Primary areas of responsibility include becoming constructively engaged in the company's affairs through strategy approval and validation; providing oversight of management to ensure the company's performance, condition, and risks are known, understood, and disclosed; ensuring the adequacy of control and information systems and compliance.

Must be prepared to devote the time required to understand the company and, based on judgment and information, to anticipate what will make it successful and what evolving risks it will face. Must be willing to challenge the CEO and management, to ask questions and assess answers objectively, to be skeptical of all information presented, to collect independent information, and to look at trade-offs from the shareholders' perspective.

Expertise in an area such as finance, audit, international operations, technology, marketing, or operations is a plus. Communication, leadership, and team-building skills are required. Must understand that while "plausible deniability" may be a legal defense, it fails to satisfy fiduciary obligations to shareholders and could very well result in public embarrassment and/or termination. Compensation commensurate with responsibility and performance.

Information given about each nominee might include not only work experience, education, and other directorships, but also anything else that could influence independence, including relationships among directors and officers or common affiliations with schools, clubs, boards, and other organizations. This is not a legal or regulatory test, and it certainly doesn't imply that all relationships are detrimental to independence. It is simply a commonsense test. The burden of disclosure is on the board and the interpretation of whether or not independence is compromised is left to shareholders.

Direct Nominations by Shareholders
Several respected governance experts have suggested that shareholders be given the right to directly nominate one or more directors by popular vote. This has already been tried in some companies, including United Airlines, now in bankruptcy, where selected directors were nominated by the union. But this solution implies that a "specially nominated" director would represent shareholders differently or better than other directors. Because all votes are equal on a board, and all directors are obligated to

represent shareholders, selecting a special interest director could tend to let other board-nominated directors off the hook as fiduciaries for all shareholders. Finally, while one outspoken director can make a difference, it takes a very unique director to voice a strong dissenting position in the face of the kind of peer pressure that exists on so many boards.

Electing—and Removing—Directors

To hold directors accountable as individuals and as a group, shareholders need a mechanism that allows them to actually vote directors into and out of office. Fundamental to the election process in a democratic society is choice among candidates. As a nation, the United States has consistently derided countries that claim to have free elections, but in practice place only one candidate for each position on the ballot. This is precisely how boards of public companies are elected.

Other respected organizations use a different process. Most colleges and universities conduct elections for trustees (the equivalent of directors) by offering voters a choice among several candidates for each seat. This model could have significant advantages for shareholders in public companies by giving them real power to actually choose their fiduciary representatives. By choosing from multiple candidates, all nominated by the board, shareholders would no longer have to vote against a nominee to make a no-confidence statement. They could actually vote in favor of the nominee they wanted.

Obviously, shareholders or the board would determine the details of such a process for a specific company. For example, if four new directors were required, a slate of eight nominees could be put forward and the four candidates receiving the most votes would prevail. Another way would be to propose two nominees for each seat and the winner would hold that seat for the term of office. Cumulative voting is yet another process that has been used in a few companies. In this model, shareholders can divide up their allotted votes in any way they see fit. For example, if five director seats are up for election, and a shareholder owns 1,000 shares, he has 5,000 votes to cast. He may cast all 5,000 for only one director, or split them up among the nominees. Thus, a minority of shareholders may be able to elect one or more directors by giving all of their votes to selected nominees.

In companies where proposals similar to those just described have been made, management often has responded that multiple candidates will "politicize" the process of director selection. They have also maintained that attracting directors would become more difficult if the nomi-

Boards should also explain to shareholders why each candidate was nominated, what expertise the candidate brings, and what makes the candidate truly independent.

nees had to face the prospect of losing an election. The first objection is simply inconsistent with the proposal. Prospective directors would not be expected to campaign among shareholders for nomination. Rather, nominating committees would nominate more than one candidate for the positions available.

Regarding the second objection, one must question whether or not qualified director candidates would feel sufficiently insecure to participate in a true election. Losing an election to a good candidate would hardly be a disgrace. The other part of the objection deserves more consideration. Finding multiple candidates for board positions might complicate the task of the nominating committee. It would necessitate a search for a greater number of qualified candidates. However, given the large number of directors sitting on multiple boards, the scarce time that these directors have available to devote to each board, and the potential conflicts that can arise from interlocking directors, shareholders would surely benefit from a broader field of qualified director candidates. Although nominating multiple candidates would complicate the nominating committee's task, the benefits to shareholders and governance could be significant.

Are there enough available, qualified director candidates? If previous experience on the board of a large company is an important qualification, the supply is definitely limited and shrinking. But it seems that might not be a critical qualification, especially given recent examples of lapses by certain boards composed of directors with considerable previous experience.

Some other concerns are more legitimate. The increasing risk to directors from plaintiff's lawsuits over lack of independence or care is likely to reduce the number of qualified candidates willing to serve, at least until this risk is mitigated. A few directors and officers (D&O) insurance providers are addressing this issue from a financial liability perspective. The real solution to the problem of shareholder lawsuits is for directors to demonstrate clearly their adherence to higher standards of loyalty and care in fulfilling their responsibilities.

If directors are to be held more accountable for their actions, they will have to work harder to fulfill their duties. With greater responsibility should come increased compensation. The benefits of fewer surprises and better governance will justify high pay for board service.

Directors Should Account for Their Decisions

Ultimately, shareholders can hold directors more accountable for their actions if they elect them and can remove them. To make informed decisions about who fulfills their fiduciary responsibilities, shareholders need more information about how well individual directors perform. Directors should disclose dissenting opinions on important issues and explain decisions that may not appear to reflect the collective will of the shareholders.

Boards are composed of more than one person presumably because shareholders and management will benefit from the wisdom, knowledge, and experience of multiple individuals with differing expertise and diverse views. Maintaining such diversity is an espoused objective of most boards. The vast majority of votes by boards, however, are unanimous, and when they are not, this fact is seldom disclosed or explained.

Issues of strategy, compliance, risk, and monitoring are complex and answers are often neither black nor white. Are shareholders to assume that after short presentations by management that directors with vastly different expertise and experience almost always agree? While the dynamics of all boardrooms differ, it is more likely that dissenting directors toe the line to show commitment and unity.

The Conference Board has recommended separate board chairman and CEO positions and that every company should have a chairman independent of management.

Such unity can be very important, especially in the short term, but at the same time shareholders deserve to know what each director really thinks. It is also true that confidentiality and competitive advantage sometimes demand that dissenting opinions are not disclosed in the short term, but longer term there is little reason why individual opinions should not be disclosed.

Each board should establish policies and procedures to disclose board votes as soon as practical. Explaining dissenting opinions and recognizing that such dissent reflects the reality of tough trade-offs doesn't show disloyalty or lack of trust in management. The logic underpinning minority views could be given by individual dissenters or as a group. Such views would not necessarily be attached to "no" votes, but could simply be used to disclose the alternatives considered and the trade-offs made. The Supreme Court has dissenting and minority opinions, as do special commissions and others.

One might realistically hope that explaining dissenting or minority views would encourage greater debate and less unanimous voting. Without explanation, dissenting votes can be interpreted as lack of loyalty. With explanation they become thoughtful views to be considered.

When boards of directors do not act in conformity with the majority will of shareholders, they have an extra obligation to explain their decision. (They, of course, run the risk of being replaced if they cannot convince shareholders, over a reasonable amount of time, that they have acted correctly.) If directors are

The objective of every widely held public company should be to have a board composed solely of independent directors other than the CEO.

convinced that they have made the right decision, they should stand by it publicly.

In practice, boards have made many decisions that have raised significant shareholder concerns. These include approving poison pill provisions to guard against hostile takeovers; paying greenmail (repurchasing stock at a premium to prevent takeover); establishing classified boards, which encourages continuity through long terms of service and staggered elections; eliminating cumulative voting; approving excessive compensation; and approving acquisitions and mergers. Even though these practices have generally served to entrench existing managements and boards, undoubtedly each may have been justified in specific instances. These practices are so troublesome because shareholders have no effective recourse against them other than expensive litigation or proxy contests, which are not economical for single shareholders.

Corporations do give shareholders an opportunity to express their will. Each proxy season shareholders vote on hundreds of proposals. Usually, management prepares these proposals, but some are prepared by shareholders. In many instances, even when a majority of shareholders has voted for or against a proposal, directors have ignored the majority will. For example, when Lucent shareholders voted to eliminate classified directors and to elect all directors annually, the board noted that although the proposal received an affirmative vote of the majority of those who voted, the total fell short of the 80 percent of all outstanding shares that would obligate the board to amend its certificate of incorporation.[1] Some shareholders have taken actions to prevent boards from disregarding the majority will. New York City Pension Funds have presented proposals to Gillette, Goodyear Tire and Rubber, and Wisconsin Energy that would force them to adopt proposals passed by a majority. Boards that continue to routinely ignore shareholder votes without explaining why may force such corrective action. At the least, the fact that shareholders are putting forth such proposals argues strongly that directors should communicate more effectively with them.

The Board/Management/CEO Relationship

As DISCUSSED AT LENGTH in Chapter 6, independence is ultimately a cultural phenomenon and an individual state of mind. There are, however, specific steps that executives and directors can take to demonstrate true independence and not just the appearance of independence. These include ensuring independent board leadership with adequate procedures and guidelines, excluding or restricting the number of the company's non-CEO executives who serve as directors, and maintaining a true and healthy system of checks and balances.

Independent Leadership

The board requires a mechanism to assure that independent directors have the opportunity and ability to set board and committee agendas, introduce concerns, determine board and committee schedules, and hold additional meetings including executive sessions (involving independent directors only). The board also needs its own independent leadership to structure presentations and coordinate the actions and findings of subcommittees.

The Conference Board recommends separate board chairman and CEO positions, and that every company should have a chairman independent of management.[2] The symbolism is tremendous. Few companies conform to this simple guideline. Among the Fortune 500 companies, 392 have the same individual serving as both CEO and chairman. Of the remaining 108 companies, only 15 have a separate chairman designated as independent. In 93 instances the chairman is separate from the CEO, but is not independent.[3] Clearly, corporate America does not agree with The Conference Board's view, and, not surprisingly, there has been considerable debate within that body's membership about it. The focus of that debate has been on separation of titles instead of on the obvious need for an independent leader on the board—the issue that The Conference Board was trying to address with a guideline.

If titles are the sticking point, everything really boils down to semantics. Having a strong, independent lead director, even if in a rotating position, addresses most of the real issues. If directors feel that the chief executive's internal or external leadership image demands both the chairman and the CEO titles, no real harm is done to governance. Companies that go that route, however, place an additional burden on the board to demonstrate effective independent leadership.

If a board decides to have a lead or presiding director, that individual must have the authority, desire, time, and resources to take on the responsibilities. No organization, including a board, is effective without leadership, and because the primary role of the board hinges on independence, the leader must be independent. The board must also ensure that independent outside directors and management work together before and after every meeting to set future agenda items, and follow up on past "to-do" items.

Independent directors should meet in executive sessions and have the ability to schedule ad hoc executive sessions as well. Such meetings are more likely to encourage directors to lay their cards on the table about sensitive issues or concerns. CEOs and other executives who are doing their jobs well and have nothing to hide should not feel apprehensive about this legitimate need. On the other hand, if the CEO is the only insider on the board and is totally committed to transparency and accountability, the need for such sessions might be dramatically reduced.

Senior Executives of the Company Should Not Be Directors

The objective of every widely held public company should be to have a board composed solely of independent directors other than the CEO. The probability of the board fulfilling its fiduciary responsibilities to shareholders is far greater with this structure than with a simple majority of independent directors.

Having senior executives on the board other than the CEO often impairs the ability of the board to oversee management and to provide constructive guidance. Because duty of care is so critical, the argument is sometimes made that senior executives must be on the board to provide information and expertise. But that benefit is available at any time without including them as voting and participating board members.

> *Monitoring is a board responsibility that adds value by routinely verifying that the processes, systems, and personnel required to track behavior are in place.*

Although the actual relationships between many boards and their CEOs appear otherwise, the CEO theoretically reports to the board. At the same time, senior executives report directly to the CEO. This can create a debilitating situation. When senior executives sit on the board, they theoretically supervise the CEO (and indirectly themselves). When they sit in a board meeting, they wear a director's hat; at all other times they report to the CEO. The implications of this conflict go far beyond the obvious fact that inside directors are not independent and cannot be expected to represent shareholders over management.

Independent directors may rightly be reluctant to seriously challenge CEOs in front of their employees. Those who argue against the separation of the CEO and board chairman roles often argue that the CEOs leadership will be challenged by the separation. If board meetings include only CEOs and independent directors this concern is largely mitigated. The ability to discuss issues more openly with the CEO at all board meetings will support and improve the CEO/board relationship. It will allow the CEO to be more open and candid with regard to senior executives, and directors can more easily challenge the CEO on issues of fact, judgment, or execution.

Investors should recognize that many companies have made a transition from entrepreneurial or privately owned businesses that were previously controlled by only a few individuals, some of whom may be major shareholders. Technology, biotech, and many financial institutions fit this description. Other companies are issuing so many options and diluting providers of capital that they have for all practical purposes become employee-owned enterprises. Investors must realistically assess the level of independence of directors, and by extension, their inclination to act as effective checks and balances on the behalf of shareholders.

Some companies maintain a simple majority of independent directors because they are in transition or because they are not particularly concerned with independence and shareholders. In such instances investors should adjust price/earnings ratios appropriately because of a possible bias in the distribution of wealth between providers of capital and labor and a higher risk of surprise events that could cause sudden declines in share prices.

Encourage Checks and Balances

The resources available to management and the power exercised daily by the CEO and senior executives dwarf those of directors. Management is accustomed to being in charge of everything. Management must recognize, however, that directors are ultimately responsible to shareholders and must not be hampered in fulfilling this responsibility.

This is where trust enters the picture. Many executives have difficulty separating the concepts of "trust" and "monitoring." Trusting management does not mean that the board ought not to monitor what management does. Monitoring is a board responsibility that adds value by routinely verifying that the processes, systems, and personnel required to track behavior and highlight potential problems are in place. Monitoring, however, should be clearly distinguished from auditing. Little added value would come from another "audit." The cost in time and distraction would not be justified by the low probability of uncovering new information.

As in any relationship, trust is earned and demonstrated through ongoing verification. The best way for management to build trust is to encourage directors to seek independent information that validates management's decisions. Having its own independent, unobtrusive information source can help give the board—and executive management for that matter—confidence that all senior personnel act within ethical and legal standards.

There's another side to trust. In many cases where management failures have had disastrous effects on shareholders, the board had every reason to trust executive leadership and did. This makes verifying through monitoring and oversight all the

> *As the shareholders' watchdog, the board must seek out problems, ask many detailed questions, and get information not supplied by management.*

more critical. As the shareholders' watchdog, the board must demonstrate great diligence in seeking out problems, ask many detailed questions, and collect and analyze information not supplied by management. If they fail in these duties, they are not fulfilling their obligation to be a deterrent to unethical behavior and fraud, nor will they have a way to know if either has occurred. The need for monitoring is not personal. It is a basic principle of good governance, and the mere fact that monitoring takes place often prevents small transgressions from becoming large problems.

Challenging Management

Even when outside information and thorough analysis raise serious questions about strategy or execution, directors may hesitate to question or challenge management. Perhaps this hesitation results from a friendship with the CEO, fear of being dismissed as a rabble-rouser, possible embarrassment when management's position is correct (which happens often), or from not wanting to waste other directors' time. None of these is a defensible position for a director who claims to represent shareholders. But directors are human. One way to enable directors to ask more probing questions would be a system by which they could voice questions or concerns anonymously through board staff members or a lead director. In that way the issues surface from the board as a whole and not from individual members.

Abiding by the True Meaning of Duty of Care

The demands that duty of care places on directors are not unreasonable when measured against directors' considerable legal and ethical responsibilities as fiduciaries. The demands

> One way to enable directors to ask more probing questions would be a system by which they could voice concerns anonymously through a lead director.

may appear unreasonable, however, when measured against the time and resources usually available to directors. In the wake of repeated scandals and business failures, lack of time, lack of information, or lack of analytical capability and knowledge are not acceptable excuses for lack of duty of care.

Directors, in fact, should devote exponentially more time—or leverage their available time through staff and experts—to meeting the standard of duty of care. This means being more diligent in collecting independently generated information, analyzing and critiquing all information (including that provided by management), fully understanding strategy, validating that the approved strategy is working, and having sufficient understanding of all details of the business to serve their checks and balances function.

The danger always exists in today's environment that management will spend too much valuable senior executive time on preparing for and orchestrating board meetings rather that on running the business. Similarly, directors could spend too much of their limited time ensuring compliance with increasing regulations and not enough time adding the value of their wisdom and experience. Both management and directors would benefit from processes and procedures that allow support staff to coordinate the exchange of information and to facilitate dialogue between the board and various levels of management.

Directors need more time. Even if directors are completely independent, the job has become too difficult to do well in what amounts to a total of fifteen to twenty-five days of work each year. Effective oversight often requires intimate knowledge of details, because incomplete or inaccurate reporting of details lies at the foundation of most of the issues and abuses that ultimately harm shareholders.

A further complication is that directors never know how much time and effort will be required. To a large extent meetings with management and with each other are defined at the beginning of each year when annual meeting schedules are determined. While it may be unfair to say that a director's time is set in stone, it is true that directors have limited flexibility to allocate more time and resources relative to the wide variation in problems they may face. When unusual issues arise, directors have very limited extra time to deal with them.

Directors need independent information. Directors need a substantial base of detailed knowledge and understanding about their company. A lot can be provided by management. But there is a constant danger that information will be filtered even before it reaches top management. Even the most honest executive may give greater weight to information that supports an existing or proposed course of action and to minimize information that is inconsistent. Even in a well-managed company, bad news seldom flows uphill, from corporate staff to CEO or from CEO to the board. This is especially true when those who have the information can justify, at least in their own minds, ignoring it, or when they feel the situation can be solved without disclosing it. Sweeping problems under the carpet, however, can lead to the slippery slope. Directors, therefore, should have their own independent information sources and analytical capability.

Boards also need the capability to organize and present alternative views to management for discussion. Ideally it would take place outside of structured board meetings. This would strengthen the board/management relationship because it would be built on trust and knowledge instead of relying on the dominance of management over directors.

To satisfy duty of care, resources given to the board should expand to meet situational demands, independently from management. Some boards may wish to hire their own staff, and have them placed away from the company's offices. The primary disadvantage of this approach is finding directors who have the time and the inclination to manage the staff. The second disadvantage is cost: A substantial staff with a broad range of expertise might be required. Alternatively it can be outsourced to one or more experts who have staff at their disposal.

> To become "real value creation" companies, it is critical that management and the board agree on the true value drivers— financial and nonfinancial— of the business.

Boards of directors often hire outside experts in limited roles. Unfortunately, it can take an inordinate amount of time for outside experts to learn about the company and sometimes they can deliver only a one-size-fits-all solution. In addition, these experts are often hired a in crisis or when an unforeseen issue arises. They have to give advice before they have had time to get intimately acquainted with the company.

A better approach might be to hire an ongoing adviser who can provide varying levels of expertise and support across the wide range of issues that the board faces regularly. In fact, the Sarbanes-Oxley Act has recognized the need for additional outside resources hired by the board instead of management. The legislation says, "The audit committee shall have the authority to engage independent counsel and other advisers, as it determines necessary to carry out its duties." An advantage of having ongoing help is that the adviser is always current on all the company's issues, its strategy, value drivers, and personalities. The adviser can also gain a detailed understanding of the company's systems, processes, and mechanisms to identify and monitor risks. This allows the adviser to understand the interrelated nature of all board issues and to offer sound information. Special purpose advisers, on the other hand, tend to focus narrowly on the issue assigned and place little weight on the ramifications and consequences of their advice on other areas. For example, compensation experts have consistently favored options for senior management and ignored or failed to understand the added responsibility this placed on directors and the audit committee (who should be guarding against earnings manufacture and monitoring stock buyback activity around stock options exercise time).

Directors need more complete, accurate information. Some argue that the primary role of directors is to assist in strategy formulation. Others argue this job is the purview of very knowledgeable executives, and that directors can provide little valuable input. In either case, directors become a more valuable asset of the business when they have greater knowledge and understanding. Management should make leveraging directors' value-added experience and wisdom a high priority by providing more complete information as well as by encouraging directors to seek out their own sources of information.

Directors need to be aware of potential legal violations. Sarbanes-Oxley requires outside legal counsel to report any evidence of material legal violations "to the company's chief legal officer, or to its chief legal officer and CEO."[4] After investigation, chief legal officers who determine a problem may exist must see that "reasonable steps" are taken by the company in response. If outside attorneys are not convinced that a report of a possible material legal violation is getting a timely and reasonable response, they must "report the evidence to an appropriate committee of the board of directors."

There are three reasons why directors should insist on knowing whenever any possible violation is reported. First, even if one defines "material" as having a substantial likelihood that a reasonable person would consider it important,[5] this rules leaves room for management to define a violation as immaterial and ignore it. Although investors might agree that the violation itself is immaterial, they might consider management's decision to ignore it as very material. Second, part of the duty of directors is to monitor the ethics of the company, and any violation goes to this responsibility. Third, why would any director in reasonably executing duty of care not wish to know of potential violations immediately? This legislation puts the burden on external lawyers to go the board if management fails to act. Is it not more appropriate for directors to put the burden on management to tell them what is going on?

Focus on Real Value Creation

If boards and management are serious about putting investors' interest first, they must make real value creation their ultimate goal and be able to demonstrate their success and report it publicly. Most companies have identified the value drivers of their business, but many do not systematically measure them, but rely instead on stock price as the primary measure of success.

To become "real value creation" companies, it is critical that management and the board agree on the true value drivers—financial and nonfinancial—of the business. Because stock price is such a poor measure of real value creation, it is incumbent on management to monitor and report on the measures that drive real value as it is created and those that serve as reasonably reliable predictors of future real value creation. It is the responsibility of the board to verify that the information is complete, accurate, and reliable.

Neither task is easy. Both require a clear and detailed understanding of corporate strategy and the priorities of strategy execution. Both depend on identifying or creating metrics for the fundamental activities that create and destroy value and systems to ensure that these activities are measured consistently from period to period. Finally, ensuring real value creation calls for a system that can correlate the results of those value creating activities with financial performance to insure that the measures and metrics chosen continue to be valid.

Align Executive Compensation With Real Value Creation

In the absence of incentive compensation based primarily on options, it is likely that executives would focus more intently on real value creation than singularly focusing on stock price appreciation. Boards that feel compelled to offer executives large amounts of incentive compensation, instead of simply paying executives handsomely, are also faced with the tasks of closely monitoring and measuring executives' effectiveness and explaining to shareholders why they feel compensation levels are appropriate. To do this properly, they would need to design and implement better long-term incentive compensation programs. Such programs ought to make the incentive compensation component a function of real value drivers rather than a function of stock price (which doesn't always correlate with management effectiveness) or of other financials that management can influence independent of real value creation.

Heavy dependence on options and equity that executives can exercise and sell while in office is difficult to justify. A good solution adopted by Jeffrey Immelt, CEO of General Electric, is his personal commitment not to sell his equity for the lesser of ten years or his departure from the company. Another solution might be to require equity held by senior management to be placed in a blind trust and managed independently, similar to requirements for stock holdings of some public officials. Although this continued stock ownership might still provide an incentive to manage stock price, having the shares managed by a trust would be a positive step. Stock-based compensation will likely not be attractive in the coming years, and directors may have to find more effective ways to truly align their interests with those of long-term shareholders.

What Lies Ahead

GETTING TO GOOD GOVERNANCE will not only take time and effort; keeping it good will also take constant vigilance. What are the chances of meaningful, sustainable change happening? The odds are only slightly better than even. Because capitalism is based on self-interest, the checks and balances required for good governance will, by definition, be tested constantly for weaknesses. Many forces will remain in play to sustain the status quo. After a flurry of "reform" activity followed by a declaration of "victory" over poor governance, all those who hope to benefit again from the Share Price Game or its next iteration will be waiting only for the next round to begin.

Insecure leaders will resist real change, offering lip service instead of action and stressing compliance with new rules and regulations as a substitute for real change. They will continue to hide behind materiality and legal compliance. They will talk about the distractions of good governance and the constraints new mechanisms place on their power and ability to serve shareholders. Politicians, who find the promise of growth at unrealistic rates an easy and attractive alternative to facing difficult trade-offs, will be natural allies in declaring "victory" over "isolated cases" of governance lapses. Their optimistic view will be bolstered by political contributions.

Assuming history is a good indicator of future performance, the prospects of real reform appear dim. Maintaining the status quo has been the ultimate outcome of every governance crisis since the 1930s. Responding to a populist call at that time, the government, not the business community, created a "solution." Designed by government, it was, of course, based less on principles than on rules and regulation. Clearly some regulations are required, but a principles-based system can only be instituted and enforced by business leaders. To date those resisting reform far outnumber those pushing for it.

On the upside, some strong forces may tip the scale toward real reform. In a condensed time frame of eight or so years, governance failures in oversight, strategy, and checks and balances contributed to a huge bubble, a significant correction, and the consequent dramatic loss of investor confidence. This is arguably the first major crisis in which the failure of checks and balances has been a primary contributing factor.

Poor strategy approval and verification contributed to the tech bubble. Poor checks and balances oversight contributed to options and compensation abuses, cooking the books to show false earnings, and obfuscation of liabilities. It appears that the broad legitimization of earnings management, often resulting in earnings manufacture, has been far more widespread than in former crises. In past crises, executives did not boast about their ability to manage earnings. A few simply committed frauds, and the argument that these were isolated problems had more credibility.

Notably, some companies that formerly led the earnings management trend are backpedaling rapidly. Perhaps most encouraging are a few select CEOs and companies that are aggressively and publicly eschewing the Share Price Game in all its manifestations. Investors can only hope that these "just in time" reforms are genuinely motivated and real, and have not been proposed just for appearance's sake.

One company that seems to have begun to move toward genuine governance reform is General Electric, under the new leadership of Jeffrey Immelt. In an interview with the authors, Immelt emphasized that GE and its board have been at the forefront of initiating policies to improve corporate governance and transparency including improving the independence of the board, appointing a presiding director, adjusting directors' compensation, accounting for options, and providing improved transparency. Immelt noted, "This is an ongoing process. GE's board will continue to consult governance experts inside and outside the company to ensure our systems, procedures, and mechanisms serve the best interests of our shareowners and our company."

Television and the press may also prove to be powerful forces on the side of reform despite the fact that the stock-market-obsessed communications media fueled the bubble, encouraged the focus on quarterly earnings, and perpetuated the Share Price Game. After all, news is news, and revelations of corporate misconduct and disastrous investor losses will make headlines. The SEC could also be a powerful force for reform after years of failing to review the financial statements and disclosure of large companies and focusing instead on hundreds of IPOs. The new leadership says it is newly committed to the bigger task and has the funding to make it happen. Time will tell. There is even some hope, although just a glimmer, that sell-side research reform may encourage real analysis of markets, technological trends, competitive advantages and disadvantages, and performance measures that indicate real value creation.

Repairing the damage of many years of systematic earnings management and manufacture and stock price manipulation will far more likely occur in an environment of real growth and productivity gains. Without the benefit of exaggerated earnings and growth, reported performance will be disappointing in the absence of a strong economy. Almost unprecedented recent monetary and fiscal stimuli may provide an economic environment allowing reform. Despite a correcting stock market, the real economy undoubtedly will recover as productivity gains continue, and corporate earnings will continue to track GDP growth. However, stocks do not generally perform well in a rising interest rate environment following protracted stimulus, so price earnings multiples may constrain a rapid rebound in prices. Widespread confidence in governance mechanisms may also be a necessary condition for the stock market's sustained recovery.

Although shareholders, executives, politicians, regulators, analysts, and the press all share responsibility for making our capital allocation system work, the onus for good governance falls ultimately on boards of directors. This book argues that everyone will benefit when boards and individual directors exercise authority with care and accept their accountability to shareholders. If boards fail to rise to the challenge, the only thing investors need to do to see what lies ahead is to look back over their shoulders at the very recent past.

NOTES

CHAPTER 1

1. The Conference Board, *The Conference Board Commission on Public Trust and Private Enterprise: Report and Recommendations,* January 9, 2003, p. 5.

2. Michael Schroeder, "Pressure on Webster is Intensifying," *The Wall Street Journal,* November 11, 2002, p. C9.

3. Steven F. Walker, "Enron: Stakeholder–Not Just Shareholder–Relations at Its Worst," StakeHolder Power (January 2002). http://www.stakeholderpower.com/story.cfm?article_id =199.

4. Leslie Wayne, "Irate Over All the Scandals, Pension Funds Go to Court," *The New York Times,* June 28, 2002. www.nytimes.com/2002/06/28/business/28PENS.html.

5. Amy Chua, *World on Fire: How Exporting Free Market Democracy Breeds Ethnic Hatred and Global Instability* (Doubleday, 2002). Cites many more examples and offers an extended and interesting discussion of these forces.

CHAPTER 2

1. Greg Ip, Kate Kelly, Joann S. Lubin, "SEC Chairman Harvey Pitt Calls for Stricter Controls Over Options," *The Wall Street Journal,* April 5, 2002.

CHAPTER 3

1. Kris Maher and Kemba J. Dunham, "Who Got the Most from Exercising Options?" *The Wall Street Journal,* December 17, 2002, sec. B, pp. 1, 3.

CHAPTER 4

1. John C. Bogle, "Don't Count on It! The Perils of Numeracy" (keynote address, *The Landmines in Finance Forum*, Center for Economic Policy Studies, Princeton University, October 18, 2002).

2. A frequent assumption is that the growth rate of dividends in the future will equal the growth rate of earnings. As explained later, this assumption is not required to validate the theory. The point here is that growth rate can be used generically to refer to growth in dividends or earnings or earnings per share with only minor adjustments.

3. Scott Thurm, "Five High Tech Companies Are Amassing Big Piles of Cash," *The Wall Street Journal*, December 27, 2002.

4. David Leonhardt and Claudia H. Deutsch, "Few Officials at Companies See a Change on Dividends," *The New York Times*, January 8, 2003, C1.

5. Ibid.

6. M. David Roberts, "Dividends: A Return to Fundamentals," Northern Trust Investments (October 2002). http://www.financial-planning.com/northerntrustinvestments/docs/divwhitepaper.pdf.

7. The arithmetic is real: 1.11 x 1.09 = 1.20099, instead of 11 + 9 = 20.

8. John C. Bogle, "Don't Count on It! The Perils of Numeracy."

9. *Financial Statement Restatements: Trends, Market Impacts, Regulatory Responses, and Remaining Challenges,* report to chairman, committee on banking, housing, and urban affairs, U.S. Senate, United States General Accounting Office, October 2002, GAO-03-138, p. 16.

CHAPTER 5

1. Gene D'Avolio with Efi Gildor and Andrei Shleifer, "Technology, Information Production, and Market Efficiency," Harvard Institute of Economic Research, Harvard University, September 18, 2001, p. 18. http://post.economics.harvard.edu/faculty/hier/2001papers/HIER1929.pdf.

2. Samuel A. DiPiazza Jr. and Robert G. Eccles, *Building Public Trust: The Future of Corporate Reporting* (New York: John Wiley & Sons, 2002), p. 40.

3. Peter Spiegel, "PwC Chief attacks audit rules," *Financial Times,* FT.com (June 18, 2002).

4. *USA Today,* June 26, 2002.

5. *Orlando Sentinel,* January 10, 2002.

6. *The Washington Post,* April 11, 2002.

7. *Times* (London), February 10, 2001.

8. *The Wall Street Journal,* June 24, 2002.

9. Alex Berenson, "Tweaking Numbers to Meet Goals Comes Back to Haunt Executives," *The New York Times,* June 29, 2002.

10. Michael R. Young, ed. *Accounting Irregularities and Financial Fraud* (New York: Aspen Law and Business, 2002), p.15.

11. Peter Keating, "Coca Cola's Secret Accounting Formula," Corporate Board Member, Summer 2000.

12. Ibid.

13. The Committee of Sponsoring Organizations of the Treadway Commission, *Fraudulent Financial Reporting: 1987–1997, An Analysis of U.S. Public Companies.* http://www.coso.org/Publications/executive_summary_fraudulent_financial_reporting.htm.

14. Thor Valdmanis, "Accounting Abracadabra: Cooking the Books Proves Common Trick of the Trade," *USA Today,* August 11, 1998, sec. B, p. 1.

15. Steve Maich, "The Ins and Outs of Stuffing Channels: Harder to Do These Days." *National Post* (Canada), November 1, 2002.

16. Jake Batsell, "Early Shipments Hound Cutter & Buck," *The Seattle Times,* August 25, 20002, sec. E, p. 1.

17. Johnathan Weil and Jathon Sapsford, "Dynegy to Pay $3 Million, Settling SEC Investigation," *The Wall Street Journal Online,* September 25, 2002.

18. Jonathan Weil, "'Cookie Jar' Trick Sweetens Earnings," *The Wall Street Journal,* November 11, 2002, p. 2.

19. Jonathan Weil, "SEC Probe of Lucent Is Broader—Inquiry Covers Possibility of Profit Manipulations Dating Back to Mid-1990s," *The Asian Wall Street Journal,* November 4, 2002, sec. A, p. 7.

20. Kathleen Day, "SEC Says Microsoft Broke Law; Company Agrees to Stop Setting Profits Aside," *The Washington Post,* June 4, 2002, sec. E, p. 1.

21. David Barboza, "Enron Reportedly Hid $1.5 Billion in Profits; State Energy Crisis Fallout Called Motive," *San Diego Union-Tribune,* June 23, 2002, sec. A, p. 1.

22. Jerry Useem, "Backward-Looking Accounting," *Fortune,* (October 28, 2002): p. 192.

23. Gretchen Morgenson, "It's Time to Move Pension Reporting Out of the Dark," *The New York Times,* November 10, 2002.

24. Robert Frank and Robin Sidel, "Firms That Lived by the Deal Are Now Sinking by the Dozens," *The Wall Street Journal,* June 6, 2002, p. 1.

25. Ibid.

26. Press release, "Vivendi Universal Reports 2001 Results," Paris, March 5, 2002.

27. Mitchell Zacks, "How Inventory Write Downs are Legal Book-Cooking," *Chicago Sun-Times,* April 29, 2001, p. 41.

28. Susan Pulliam and Deborah Solomon, "Uncooking the Books: How Three Unlikely Sleuths Discovered Fraud at WorldCom," *The Wall Street Journal,* October 30, 2002, sec. A, p. 1.

29. "Were Profits Inflated?" *Business Week* (March 4, 2002): p. 14.

30. Sarah Ellison, "P&G Scrubs Use of Special Items in Restructuring," *The Wall Street Journal,* December 13, 2002, B7.

31. "Out, by $100 Billion," *The Economist* (February 21, 2002).

32. Jennifer Caplan, "Buybacks or Giveaways," CFO.com, September 20, 2002.

33. Ibid.

34. "Some Insiders Cashed in on IBM Stock's Rise, Buybacks," *Annex Bulletins* (May 1997).

35. "Xerox to Buy Tektronic Color-Printing Unit for $950 Million," Dow Jones Business News, Dow Jones Interactive, September 22, 1999.

36. Keith H. Hammonds, "The Secret Life of the CEO: Do They Even Know Right from Wrong?" *Fast Company* (December 31, 2002).

37. U.S. Securities and Exchange Commission, "Xerox Settles SEC Enforcement Action Charging Company With Fraud," Litigation Release No. 17465, April 11, 2002.

38. U.S. Securities and Exchange Commission, "Xerox Settles SEC Enforcement Action Charging Company With Fraud," news release, April 11, 2002.

39. William M. Bulkeley, "Ex-Xerox Officials Got Big Bonuses Despite SEC's Accounting Concerns," *The Wall Street Journal,* April 19, 2002.

40. Julie E. Satow, "Underfunded Pension Plans May Prompt COs to Market," *Corporate Financing Week* (January 5, 2003).

CHAPTER 6

1. Arthur Levitt with Paula Dwyer, *Take on the Street: What Wall Street and Corporate America Don't Want You to Know* (New York: Pantheon Books, 2002), 204–205.

2. William James Durant, Will Durant, and Ariel Durant, *The Lessons of History* (New York: Simon & Schuster, August 1968).

3. Thomas A. Stewart, "The King is Dead," *Fortune* (January 14, 1993).

4. Jerry Useem, "From Heroes to Goats … and Back Again? How Corporate Leaders Lost Our Trust," *Fortune* (November 3, 2002).

5. Alan Ehrenhalt, "The Paradox of Corrupt Yet Effective Leadership," *The New York Times,* September 30, 2002, A23.

6. Ibid.

7. Joseph Blasi, Douglas Kruse, and Aaron Bernstein, *In the Company of Owners: The Truth about Stock Options (and Why Every Employee Should Have Them)* (New York: Basic Books, 2003).

8. Richard Gibson, "Buffett Warns about Derivatives," *The Wall Street Journal,* March 4, 2003, C3.

9. The Conference Board, *The Conference Board Commission on Public Trust and Private Enterprise: Findings and Recommendations,* January 9, 2003, p.17.

10. Marc Gunther, "Investors of the World: Unite!," *Fortune* (June 24, 2002).

CHAPTER 7

1. "The Best & Worst Boards: Our New Report Card on Corporate Governance," *Business Week* (November 25, 1996).

2. "The Best and Worst Boards: Our Special Report on Corporate Governance," *Business Week* (December 8, 1997).

3. "The Best and Worst Corporate Boards," Special Report, Corporate Governance, *Business Week* (January 24, 2000).

4. "The Best and Worst Boards: How the Corporate Scandals Are Sparking a Revolution in Governance," *Business Week* (October 7, 2002).

5. David Henry with Heather Timmons, "Still Spinning the Numbers," *Business Week* (November 11, 2002).

6. Charles Peck, Henry Silvert, and Gina McCormick, *Directors' Compensation and Board Practices in 2001,* The Conference Board, pp. 20–21.

7. Jeffrey Sonnenfeld, "Introducing the Watchdogs for Corporate Governance," *The Wall Street Journal,* March 11, 2003.

8. PricewaterhouseCoopers, "Sarbanes-Oxley Act Requires Changes in Corporate Control, Compliance," Barometer Surveys release, March 24, 2003. http://www.barometersurveys.com.

9. Bruce Orwall, "Disney Board Braces for Impact of New Independence Standards," *The Wall Street Journal Online,* August 12, 2002.

10. Louis Lavelle, "Disney: More Insiders at the Castle," *BusinessWeek Online* (February 14, 2003).

11. Jeffrey Sonnenfeld, "What Makes Great Boards Great," *Harvard Business Review* (September 2002): p. 106.

12. Robert A. G. Monks and Nell Minow, *Corporate Governance* (Oxford: Blackwell Publishers Ltd., Second Edition, 2001), p. 168.

13. Ibid.

14. *Abbott v. American Hard Rubber Co.,* 33 Barbour 578.

15. National Association of Corporate Directors, *Report of the NACD Blue Ribbon Commission on Audit Committees: A Practical Guide,* 2000 Edition, p. 10. Also see: www.nacdonline.org.

16. The Business Roundtable, "Principles of Corporate Governance," May 2002. Also see: www.brt.org.

17. Adolf A. Berle and Gardiner C. Means, *The Modern Corporation & Private Property* (New Brunswick, N.J.: Transaction Publishers, Fourth Printing, 2002), p. 205.

18. Investor Protection Association, Corporate Governance in Russia, http://www.corp-gov.org/projects/indep.php3.

19. Berle and Means, p. 202.

20. *Hun v. Cary,* 82 N.Y. 65, 1880.

21. *Railroad Co v. Lockwood,* 17 Wall, 357, 382 (United States Supreme Court).

22. Berle and Means, p. 203.

23. *Graham v. Allis Chalmers Manufacturing Co.,* 188 A.2d 125 (Del. 1963).

24. "The Best & Worst Boards: Our New Report Card on Corporate Governance," *Business Week* (November 25, 1996).

25. Jerry Useem, "In Corporate America It's Cleanup Time," *Fortune* (September 16, 2002).

CHAPTER 8

1. Notice of 2003 Annual Meeting and Proxy Statement, Lucent Technologies.

2. The Conference Board, *The Conference Board Commission on Public Trust and Private Enterprise: Report and Recommendations,* January 9, 2003, p. 5.

3. The Corporate Library, "Exclusive Special Report on CEO/Chairman Splits in the S&P 500: How Many and How Independent?," http://www.thecorporatelibrary.com/spotlight/boardsanddirectors/SplitChairs.html.

4. Final Rule 33-8177, Release Nos. 34-47235, File No. S7-40-02. Effective March 3, 2003.

5. Risk Oversight—Report of the NACD Blue Ribbon Commission (Washington, D.C.: NACD, 2002) p. 55.

INDEX

ABOUT BLOOMBERG

BLOOMBERG L.P., founded in 1981, is a global information services, news, and media company. Headquartered in New York, the company has nine sales offices, two data centers, and 87 news bureaus worldwide. Bloomberg, serving customers in 126 countries around the world, holds a unique position within the financial services industry by providing an unparalleled range of features in a single package known as the BLOOMBERG PROFESSIONAL™ service. By addressing the demand for investment performance and efficiency through an exceptional combination of information, analytic, electronic trading, and Straight Through Processing tools, Bloomberg has built a worldwide customer base of corporations, issuers, financial intermediaries, and institutional investors.

BLOOMBERG NEWS®, founded in 1990, provides stories and columns on business, general news, politics, and sports to leading newspapers and magazines throughout the world. BLOOMBERG TELEVISION®, a 24-hour business and financial news network, is produced and distributed globally in seven different languages. BLOOMBERG RADIO℠ is an international radio network anchored by flagship station BLOOMBERG® 1130 (WBBR-AM) in New York.

In addition to the BLOOMBERG PRESS® line of books, Bloomberg publishes *BLOOMBERG® MARKETS* and *BLOOMBERG® WEALTH MANAGER*. To learn more about Bloomberg, call a sales representative at:

Frankfurt:	49-69-92041-0	São Paulo:	55-11-3048-4500
Hong Kong:	852-2977-6900	Singapore:	65-6212-1000
London:	44-20-7330-7500	Sydney:	61-2-9777-8601
New York:	1-212-318-2200	Tokyo:	81-3-3201-8900
San Francisco:	1-415-912-2970		

FOR IN-DEPTH MARKET information and news, visit the Bloomberg website at **WWW.BLOOMBERG.COM**, which draws from the news and power of the BLOOMBERG PROFESSIONAL® service and Bloomberg's host of media products to provide high-quality news and information in multiple languages on stocks, bonds, currencies, and commodities.

ABOUT THE AUTHORS

SCOTT C. NEWQUIST is president and cofounder of Board Governance Services, Inc., an advisory firm devoted exclusively to assisting corporate boards of directors in researching, analyzing, and addressing the many issues and challenges they face in exercising their considerable duties and to work more effectively with management to enhance long-term shareholder value. He is also cofounder and chairman of Advisory Capital Partners, Inc., which works with companies to provide merger and acquisition, financial, strategic, and implementation advice.

From 1989 to 1992, he was executive managing director of Kidder Peabody and Company, a subsidiary of General Electric Company, responsible for all of that firm's investment banking activities and client relationships. Previously, he served at Morgan Stanley & Company in various roles including managing director in charge of merchant banking, managing director in charge of M&A new business development, and M&A transaction specialist. Before joining Morgan Stanley, Mr. Newquist was an officer of Morgan Guaranty Trust, specializing in high technology. He received his M.B.A. from Harvard Business School, where he was a George F. Baker Scholar, and his B.A. from Williams College, where he was elected to Phi Beta Kappa.

MAX B. RUSSELL is a professional writer and a member of Arc Group Ltd., a Chicago-based corporate communications firm. He most recently collaborated on *Building Public Trust: The Future of Corporate Reporting* with authors Sam DiPiazza, Jr., CEO of PricewaterhouseCoopers and Robert G. Eccles, president of Advisory Capital Partners. He also collaborated on *The Value Reporting Revolution: Moving Beyond the Earnings Game* with authors Robert G. Eccles, E. Mary Keegan, Robert H. Herz, and David M. H. Phillips and on *Balanced Sourcing: Cooperation and Competition in Supplier Relationships* with Timothy Laseter, vice president of Booz Allen Hamilton. In addition, Mr. Russell has written extensively on professional ethics, corporate social responsibility, business operations, risk management, and other business issues. He holds an M.B.A. from Northwestern University's Kellogg School of Management.